ᴇᴀꜱʏ TO MAKE
TEDDY BEARS

EASY TO MAKE
TEDDY BEARS
Jill Plank

ANAYA PUBLISHERS LTD LONDON

First published in Great Britain in 1993
by Anaya Publishers Ltd, Strode House, 44-50 Osnaburgh Street,
London NW1 3ND

Editor Eve Harlow
Design by Design 23
Photography Steve Tanner
Illustrations and patterns Terry Evans

British Library Cataloguing in Publication data

Plank, Jill
Easy to make teddy bears.–(Easy to make series)
I. Title II. Series
ISBN 1 85470-030-8

Typeset by Servis Filmsetting Ltd, Manchester UK.
Colour Reproduction by Scantrans Pte Ltd, Singapore.
Produced by Mandarin Offset.
Printed and bound in Hong Kong.

CONTENTS

Introduction

For children, one of the best-loved of all toys is the teddy bear. Many adults still have a cherished bear from their childhood. This book introduces you to a whole new family of bears.

Making teddy bears is a hobby I discovered quite by accident, several years ago. I have always loved and treasured bears and craved an 'antique' bear. Those I saw on sale were far too expensive for me. Then a friend gave me a paper pattern for a traditional teddy bear and I decided to try and adapt the design, to look more like the bear I wanted. As a complete novice to toymaking, I was blissfully unaware of what I was letting myself in for. I made many mistakes – and wasted a great deal of fur fabric – before I completed my first, hand-made bear. The pleasure and pride I felt in my creation cannot be described. The bear had a lopsided face and a quizzical expression – but I loved him – and he was the incentive to my continuing to make teddy bears.

Now, several years later, I have made over a hundred bears, some for myself, others as gifts for family and friends.

From that first bear, different styles have evolved. I found that by changing the size of the eyes or the shape of the nose and mouth, I could make a grumpy bear cheerful or a frankly boyish bear look like a little lady! I discovered the secrets of positioning eyes correctly (one of the most critical aspects of making bears) so that the finished toy had instant appeal. And, perhaps most important, I evolved design 'tricks' that made my bears incredibly easy to make. You will find all my secrets in this book.

Once you start making teddy bears as a hobby, you will find that the word goes round your family and circle of friends quite quickly. Nephews and nieces begin asking for their 'own' bears, at Christmas and for birthdays. Older family members and friends either want a bear for themselves, or want one for *their* friends. I can hardly keep pace with the demand – and so it will be for you. My home is now continually littered with half-made bears, limbs, heads and bodies, awaiting assembly, and what started as an experiment for a bear I particularly

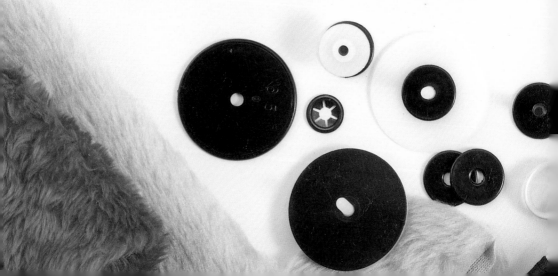

wanted has now become an absorbing hobby.

Recently, I find that I enjoy designing new bears more than re-making the old favourites and I love seeing how the particular bear character evolves from just fur fabric, stuffing and eyes and nose. I am never quite sure who is going to appear on my work table!

Old and new favourites

My very first bear design is in this book – the Edwardian bear on page 52. I still have the original. This design has jointed limbs and, although I have simplified the making, I would not advise an absolute beginner to start with this bear. Instead, choose one of the bears from the first chapter, Simple bears. Here you will find easy patterns such as the Blanket bear and Charlie, or the little bears, Tiny Tim and the Mini-bears. After making one or two from this chapter, try making the Polar bear or Chubby bear – both very straightforward designs. You might then feel confident enough to progress to the Sweetheart bear (a lovely gift for a friend) or even Great-uncle Humphrey! This large bear has a great deal of character.

I have included some bears made of fabrics other than fur – the Tartan twins for instance (ideal gifts for Scottish friends, or as unusual New Year presents). Bathtime bear, on page 20, is made of washable cotton towelling while Velvety bear is made of soft, blue velvet. Other kinds of fabrics can be used – cotton jersey is good, and so is furnishing plush. Trying out different kinds of fabrics adds to the fun of the craft.

I decided to put some less usual types of bears into the book. In the Special bears chapter, you will find Get well bear, designed especially to cheer up sick friends. Bedtime bear is a pyjama/nightie case that can have a hotwater bottle popped inside on cold nights for a warming cuddle.

I have included a Beanbag bear – children will love him – but please empty the beans out before you wash the toy. If the filling is left inside, you may find yourself with cooked beans! And, again for children, there is a bear puppet.

As you see, there is something for everyone in this book – bears to collect, bears to love and cuddle and bears to play with. And you, the bear creator, will find that there is almost nothing to equal the pleasure you will get from making a unique teddy bear – and then presenting it to someone who will love your creation for always.

ONE

Simple Bears

Tiny Tim

This bear is a quick pattern to make up and the perfect size for a small child's hands but choose a washable fabric if the toy is to be laundered frequently.

Materials

Tracing pattern paper
10in (25cm) of wool fabric 36in (90cm)
  wide   -
10in (25cm) square of brown felt
Pair of ¼in (6mm)-diameter amber-
  coloured safety eyes
Washable polyester toy filling
Dark brown stranded embroidery cotton
Narrow cord for a bow (optional)

Preparation

1 Trace the pattern pieces and put in all words, numerals and marks. Cut out the pattern pieces.

2 Pin the pattern pieces to the fabric, reversing pieces for right and left sides. Cut out 1 back on the fold, 2 fronts and 2 ears, taking note of the directional arrows on the pattern. Cut 2 ears from felt. Transfer the pattern markings onto the fabric.

Making the toy

3 Insert the safety eyes in the positions marked on the pattern.

4 Stitch pairs of ears together, fabric to felt and right sides facing (C – D), leaving the straight edges open. Turn the ears right side out.

5 Stitch the front body pieces together (A – B).

6 Baste the made-up ears to the right side of the front in the positions marked on the pattern, matching raw edges and making sure that the felt side is downwards. (This ensures that the felt side faces fowards when the bear is made up.) Baste the back to the front, right sides facing.

7 Right sides facing, stitch the back and front together (A – B – A) leaving a 2in (5cm) gap in the seam between the legs for stuffing. Turn the body right side out.

8 Stuff the toy firmly. Close the open seam with ladder stitches.

9 Embroider the nose and mouth using 3 strands of embroidery cotton.

10 Tie a cord bow round the bear's neck and sew in place.

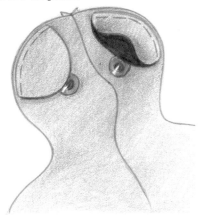

Baste the ears to the front piece, felt side down.

People who love teddy bears are *arctophiles* from the Greek word *arktos* – bear and *philos* meaning friend. The first teddy bear is said to have made in 1902 in the USA by Morris Michtom.

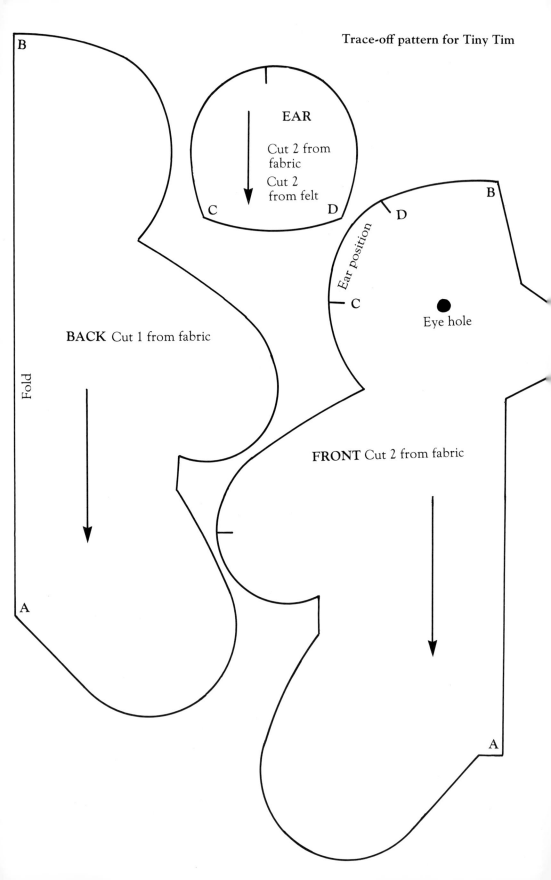

Trace-off pattern for Tiny Tim

B

EAR

Cut 2 from fabric

Cut 2 from felt

C   D

D

B

Ear position

C

Eye hole

BACK Cut 1 from fabric

Fold

FRONT Cut 2 from fabric

A

A

Charlie

This little bear would make an ideal present for a young child. The legs and arms are part of the main body so there are no tricky seams to worry about.

Materials
Squared pattern paper
12in (30cm) of cream-coloured fur fabric
   36in (90cm) wide
Pair of ¼in (6mm)-diameter brown safety
   eyes
Washable polyester toy filling
Dark brown stranded embroidery cotton

Preparation
1 Draw the graph pattern on squared
pattern paper.

2 Put in all words, numerals and marks.
Cut out the paper pattern pieces.

3 Pin the pattern pieces to the wrong
side of the fur fabric, taking note of the
directional arrows on the pattern and
reversing pieces for left and right sides.

4 Cut out 2 heads, 1 gusset, 2 backs, 1
front (on the fold of fabric) and 4 ear
pieces. Transfer the pattern markings
onto the fabric.

Making the toy
5 Stitch the heads together, right sides
facing (F – G).

6 Baste and then stitch the gusset
between the head pieces, right sides
facing (D – G, G – D), leaving a ⅛in (3mm)
gap in the seams (see pattern) for the eyes
pegs. Turn the head right side out.

7 Stitch the back body pieces together,
right sides facing (C – D), leaving a 2in
(5cm) gap in the seam for turning.

8 Stitch front and backs together along
the top of the arms (E – Y).

9 Insert and baste the head into the body
cavity, right sides facing, matching the
head to the front body at F and at the
back at D. Stitch the head to the body.

10 Stitch the front and back together all
round (Y – C – Y).

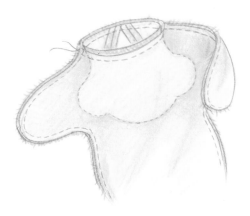

Insert and stitch the head to the body.

11 Turn the bear right side out through
the gap in the seam.

12 Insert the safety eyes in the head and
secure with washers.

13 Stuff the bear very firmly and close
the open seam with ladder stitches.

14 Stitch pairs of ears together, right
sides facing, leaving the straight edge
open. Turn right side out. Turn a narrow
hem and then oversew the straight edges
together. Ladder-stitch the ears to the
head.

15 Embroider the nose and mouth using
3 strands of embroidery cotton.

Basting (tacking)
When joining two pieces of fabric
it is advisable to baste or tack
them together first. This ensures
that both layers of fabric are fed
through the sewing machine at the
same pace, avoiding one layer
creeping or stretching. To baste,
knot the thread end and work ½in
(1cm)-long running stitches along the
stitching line, taking stitches through
both layers of fabric. Use a
contrasting thread. To remove after
stitching, clip the knot and pull the
thread through.

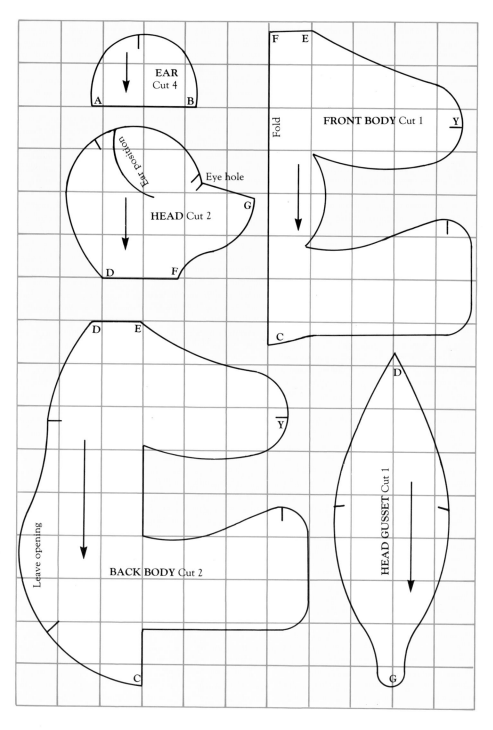

EAR Cut 4

A B

Ear position

Eye hole

HEAD Cut 2

G

D F

F E

Fold

FRONT BODY Cut 1 Y

C

D E

Y

Leave opening

BACK BODY Cut 2

C

D

HEAD GUSSET Cut 1

G

Scale: 1 sq = 1in (2.5cm)

15

Blanket bear

Here is a bear that anyone can make, even if you have not tried toy-making before. There are just the front and back body pieces, ears and a muzzle – so it could not be simpler!

Materials
Squared pattern paper
24in (60cm) of blanket-type fabric 36in
(90cm) wide
10in (25cm) square of beige felt
Pair of ⅜in (9mm)-diameter safety eyes
Small safety nose
Washable polyester toy filling

Preparation
1 Draw the graph pattern on squared pattern paper.

2 Put in all the words, numerals and marks.

3 Pin the pattern pieces to the fabric. From fabric, cut out 1 front on fold, 1 back on fold and 2 back ear pieces. From felt cut 2 front ear pieces and 1 muzzle on the fold. Transfer the pattern markings.

Making the toy
4 Stitch the darts on the front piece (A – B) leaving a ⅛in (3mm) gap for the eye pegs (see pattern).

5 Stitch the head darts on the back piece (A – B). Stitch the dart (E) in the front ear pieces.

6 Stitch the blanket fabric ears to the felt ears, right sides facing, along the curved, notched edge (F – G). Turn the ears right side out.

7 Baste the ears to the front body piece, matching points F and G. (Make sure the felt side faces forwards.)

8 Stitch the body pieces together, right sides facing (C – H – I – J – I – H – C –

C), leaving an opening in a seam for turning.

9 Overstitch the legs at each side (J) by ½in (1cm).

10 Stitch up the darts in the front piece at the arms. Turn right side out.

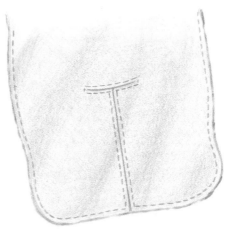

Overstitch at each side of the legs.

11 Stitch the muzzle together, right sides facing (K – L) leaving a ⅛in (3mm) gap for the nose peg (L). Turn right side out. Insert the nose and secure with a washer.

12 Baste the muzzle on the front of the bear (see picture). Oversew in place, leaving a gap at the bottom for stuffing. Stuff the muzzle firmly and close the opening with oversewing.

13 Insert the eyes and secure with the washers.

14 Stuff the bear firmly and close the seam with ladder stitches.

17

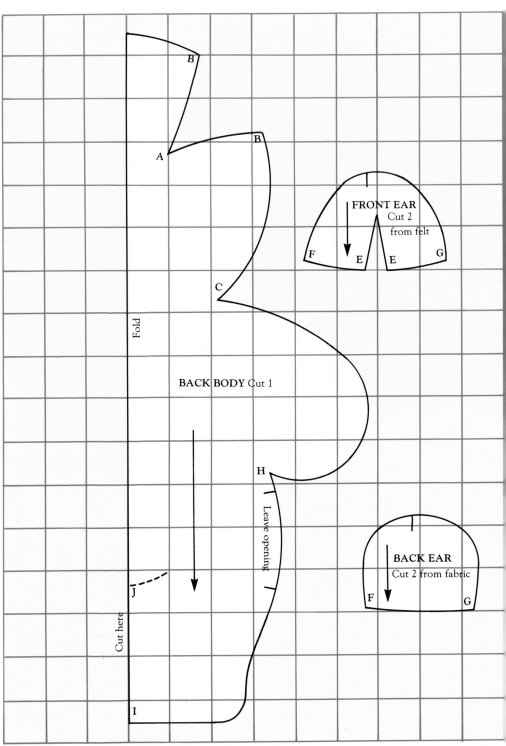

FRONT EAR
Cut 2
from felt

F E E G

BACK BODY Cut 1

Fold

Leave opening

Cut here

BACK EAR
Cut 2 from fabric

F G

Scale: 1 sq = 1in (2.5cm)

18

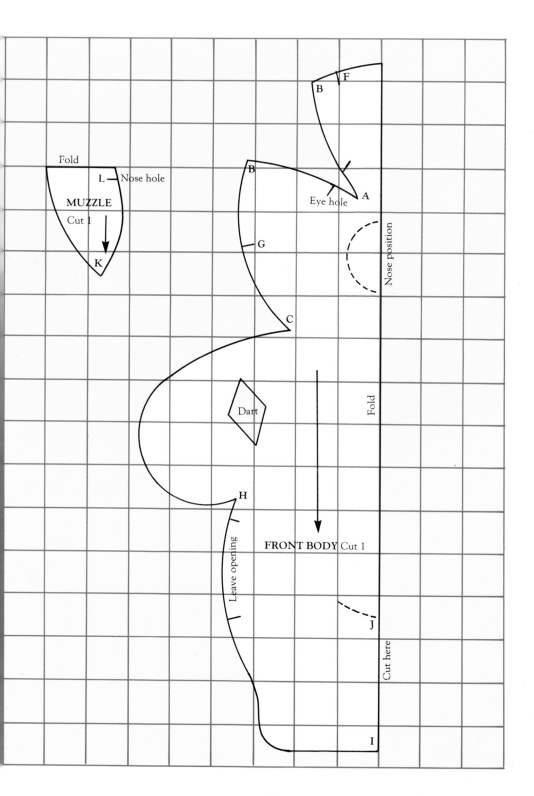

Fold

L — Nose hole

MUZZLE

Cut 1

K

B F

B

Eye hole A

Nose position

G

C

Dart

Fold

H

Leave opening

FRONT BODY Cut 1

J

Cut here

I

Bathtime bear

A small, friendly bear made of washable towelling that will encourage small children to feel that bath time can also be play time. The design can also be made up in cotton velour.

Materials

Tracing paper

10in (25cm) of cotton towelling 36in (90cm) wide

Pair of small safety eyes with plastic washers

Washable polyester toy filling

Fabric for a scarf (optional)

Preparation

1 Trace the pattern and put in all words, numerals and marks. Cut out the pattern pieces.

2 Pin the pattern to the fabric and cut 1 back and 1 front on the fold of fabric. On the front body piece, cut from A – C (on the fold) and from A – Y. Cut 4 ears. Cut 1 muzzle on the fold of fabric. Transfer the pattern markings onto the fabric.

Making the toy

3 Stitch the muzzle into the front head, right sides facing (A – C – A).

4 Stitch 2 pairs of ears, right sides facing (D – E), leaving the shorter, curved edge unstitched. Turn right sides out and oversew the open edges together.

5 Baste the ears to the right side of the front in the positions shown on the pattern.

6 Cut the front and back body pieces along F – G to form legs.

7 Baste back to front, right sides facing. Stitch all round the head and limbs, leaving a gap for turning.

8 Over-stitch the seams for about ½in (1cm) under the arms and at the top of the legs to give the limbs more shape.

9 Stitch the muzzle seam (B – A – Y).

10 Insert the eyes. Turn the bear right side out and stuff softly. Close the open seam with ladder stitches. Make a scarf if desired.

Cut the front and back body pieces to form legs.

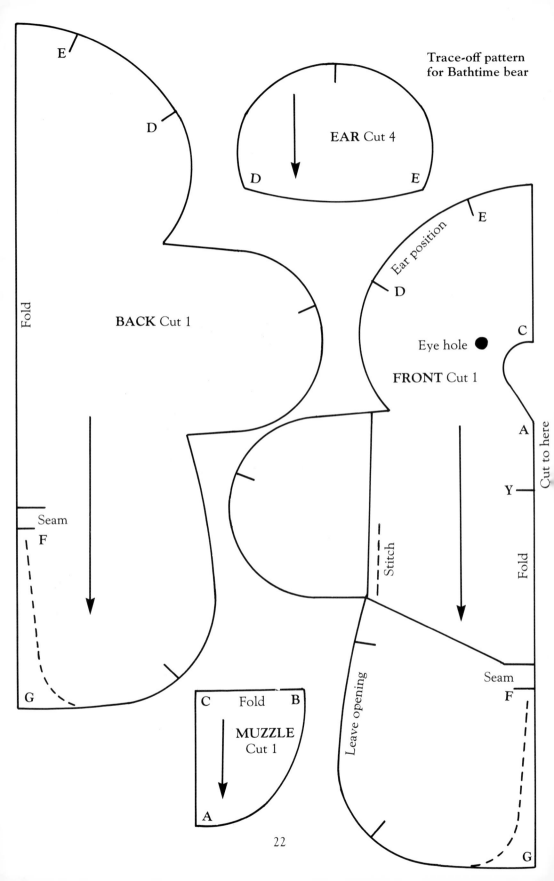

Trace-off pattern
for Bathtime bear

E

D

EAR Cut 4

D   E

E

Ear position

D

Eye hole ●

C

FRONT Cut 1

Fold

BACK Cut 1

A

Cut to here

Y

Fold

Seam

F

Stitch

Leave opening

Seam

F

G

C   Fold   B

MUZZLE
Cut 1

A

G

22

Handy puppet

Hand puppets are always fun to play with and children are especially good at manipulating them. This is a very easy pattern to use and no difficult sewing is involved.

Materials

Squared pattern paper
15in (37.5cm) of yellow felt 36in (90cm)
   wide
10in (25cm) square of black felt
Pair of $\frac{3}{8}$in (9mm)-diameter safety eyes
1 small safety nose
Washable polyester toy filling

Preparation

1 Draw the graph pattern on squared
paper. Put in all words, numerals and
marks. Cut out the pattern pieces.

2 Pin the patterns to the felt, reversing
pieces for right and left sides. From
yellow felt, cut 2 body pieces (1 back, 1
front), 2 ears, 1 back head on the fold, 1
front head on the fold and 2 finger pieces
for inside the head. From black felt, cut 2
ears, 1 muzzle and 2 paw pads. Transfer
the pattern markings onto the fabrics.

Making the toy

3 Stitch the black ears to the yellow ears
along the curved, notched edge (A – B).
Turn right side out.

4 Stitch the darts in the front head piece
(C – D). Stitch the darts in the back head
piece (E – F).

5 Baste the ears to the right side of the
front head piece (see pattern) making sure
that the black side faces forwards.

6 Stitch the front and back head pieces
together, right sides facing (G – H – G).
Turn right side out.

7 Stitch the muzzle along I – J, leaving a
$\frac{1}{8}$in (3mm) gap at J for the nose peg. Turn
the muzzle right side out. Insert the nose
and secure with the washer.

8 Baste the muzzle to the front head
piece. Sew in place with tiny oversewing
stitches, leaving a $\frac{1}{2}$in (1cm) opening at the
base for stuffing.

9 Stuff the muzzle firmly. Close the seam
with oversewing.

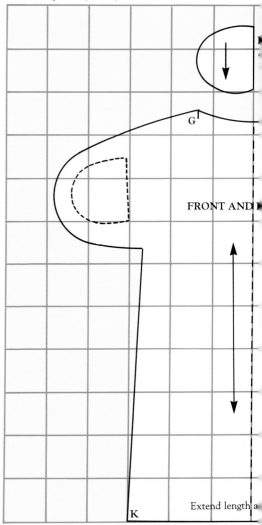

Scale: 1 sq = 1in (2.5cm)

G

FRONT AND

Extend length a

K

10 Pierce holes in the front head for the
eyes (see pattern). Insert the eyes and
secure with washers.

11 Stitch the front and back body
together at the sides (G – K).

12 Insert the head into the body cavity,
right sides facing, matching points G at
each side. Stitch. Turn right side out.

13 Stuff the head firmly, making sure
that you can get your middle and index
fingers well up into the cavity. Check that

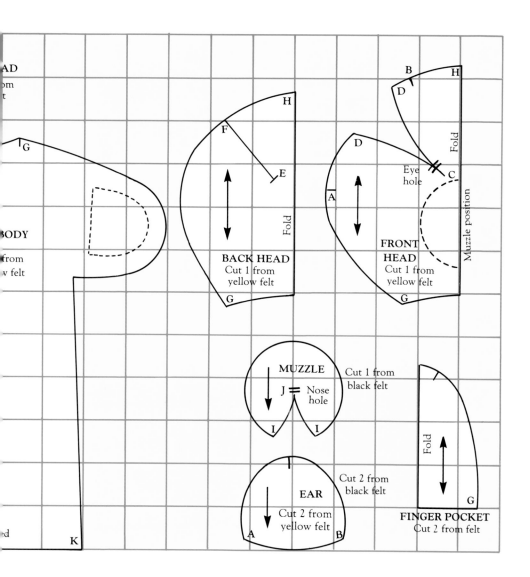

the head is evenly stuffed by pulling the body to the right side and viewing the head then pull the body back up over the head.

14 Stitch the finger pieces together along the curved, notched side (G – G). Stitch the finger piece to the head neck seam, matching points G on each side. Ease the finger piece up into the head cavity and turn the body right side out.

15 Baste the paw pads to the front body piece (see pattern). Oversew the pads to

the paws but leaving a small gap for stuffing. Stuff the pads lightly and close the opening.

Threads and yarns
Use all-purpose sewing thread for both machine-stitching and hand sewing, making sure that the colour closely matches the body fabrics.

For working noses and mouths, use stranded embroidery cotton, Persian tapestry wool or buttonhole twist.

Beanbag bear

The children will have great fun tossing this bear about but take the beans out before washing the toy or they may cook! If you prefer, the bear can be stuffed.

Materials
Squared pattern paper
Washable fur fabric, 10 × 36in
  (25 × 90cm)
Brown felt, 10in (25cm) square
Pair of ¼in (6mm)-diameter safety eyes
Small safety nose
Dried beans, peas or lentils

Preparation
1 Draw the graph pattern on squared pattern paper. Put in all words, numerals and marks. Cut out the pattern pieces.

2 Pin the pattern pieces to the wrong side of the fabric, taking note of the directional arrows on the pattern. Cut out 1 back piece on the fold of fabric, 2 front pieces, 2 ear pieces. Transfer the pattern markings onto the fabric.

3 Pin the muzzle pattern to folded felt and cut out. Cut 2 ear pieces from single felt.

Making the toy
5 Stitch the 2 fronts together (A – B and C – D).

6 Make up 2 pairs of ears, stitching fur to felt and right sides facing, leaving G – H open. Turn right side out and oversew along G – H. Baste the ears to the front head in the positions marked on the pattern, the felt side downwards. (This ensures that the felt side of the ears faces forwards when the bear is made up.)

7 Baste the back to the front, right sides facing. Stitch front to back from A, all round through D to A, leaving a 2in (5cm) gap in the seam for stuffing.

8 Stitch the curved edges of the muzzle together (B – F) leaving a ⅛in (3mm) gap in the seam at F for the nose peg (see pattern).

9 Stitch the muzzle into the head (B – C – B) right sides facing.

10 Insert the safety nose and eyes into the head in the positions marked on the pattern, working on the wrong side. Turn right side out.

11 Make a paper cone and fill the bear with dried beans. Sew up the seam with ladder stitches.

Pattern templates
If you are going to use a soft toy pattern more than once, it is a good idea to cut templates. Trace the paper pattern onto strong card. Transfer all the marks, words, numerals and pattern instructions. Cut out the template very carefully. Make sure that you have clearly identified the various pieces as belonging to the same toy as one ear looks very like another!
  To use the templates, position them on the wrong side of the fabric and trace round with a soft pencil or chalk pencil.

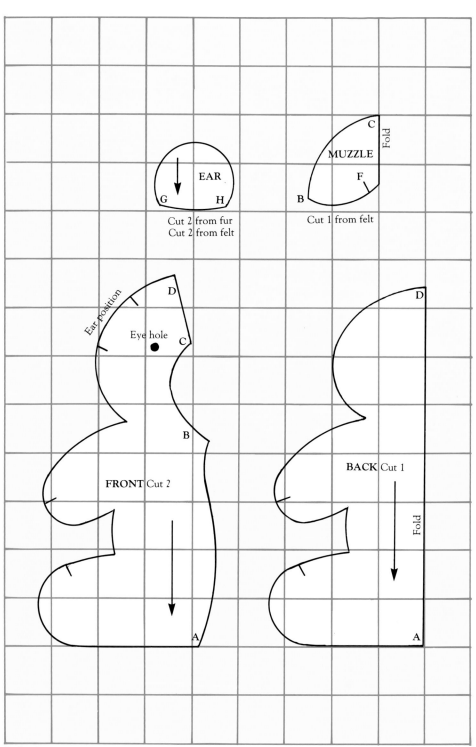

EAR

G   H

Cut 2 from fur
Cut 2 from felt

C Fold

MUZZLE

F

B

Cut 1 from felt

Ear position

Eye hole ● C

D

B

FRONT Cut 2

A

D

BACK Cut 1

Fold

A

Scale: 1 sq = 1in (2.5cm)

Great little bears

These dear little toys will make marvellous mascots – you could knit a miniature club scarf for each bear. The arms and legs are movable, strung on elastic threads passed through the body.

Materials

Tracing pattern paper
12in (30cm) square of felt (for each bear)
Washable polyester toy filling
Shirring elastic
Black (or brown) stranded embroidery
  cotton

Preparation

1 Trace the pattern pieces, putting in all the words, numerals and marks. Cut out the pattern pieces and pin to the fabric.

2 Cut 1 head piece on the fold of fabric, 2 ears, 2 body pieces, 4 arm pieces, and 2 leg pieces cut on the fold of fabric. Cut the slit A – B on the head piece.

Making the toy

3 Note that all seams are joined using tiny oversewing stitches, worked on the **wrong** side, unless otherwise stated. Insert the ears in the slits A – B on the head piece and sew in place.

4 Sew the head seams, right sides facing, (ie, with the ears on the inside) C – D, G – D on both sides of the head, and then E – F. Turn right side out.

5 Sew the darts in the body pieces H – I.

6 Sew the body pieces together C – H – E leaving a 2in (5cm) gap at the back.

7 Insert the head in the body cavity and, taking a ¼in (6mm) seam allowance at the neck edge, and right sides facing, machine-stitch (or back-stitch) the head to the body E – C – E.

8 Turn the bear to the right side and stuff the head firmly.

9 Sew the arm pieces together in pairs, right sides facing, leaving a 1in (2.5cm) gap in the seam for stuffing. Turn the arms right side out and stuff them firmly. Close the open seams with ladder stitches.

> **Bears for Christmas**
> Here is a new idea for Christmas tree decoration using small teddy bears. Make several felt bears, either all in white felt or in bear colours – grey, brown, black etc. (White looks most decorative but the felt colour is optional.) Tie on a neck bow of gold or red gift ribbon round each bear's neck. Fasten a gold thread hanger to the neck ribbon and hang the bears from the tree branches. For extra colour, a big bow of crushed paper ribbon can be tied to the branch behind each bear.

10 Sew the seam up on the legs, right sides facing, (J – K) leaving 1in (2.5cm) gaps in the seam for stuffing. Turn the legs right side out and stuff firmly. Close the open seams with ladder stitches.

11 Fixing on the limbs Thread a strong, long needle with shirring elastic, pull the ends level and knot. Entering the body through the back opening of the bear, push the needle through the marked arm position then into the corresponding mark on the arm. Take a stitch in the arm then pass the needle back through the body to the opposite side of the bear. Attach the other arm in the same way, taking the elastic back into the body cavity. Tie the elastic ends together inside the bear so that there is a little 'give'.

12 Attach the legs in the same way.

13 Stuff the body solidly, working stuffing all round the elastic joints. Close the back opening with ladder stitches.

14 Working from the picture, embroider the eyes and nose in satin stitch. Work the line under the nose and the mouth in back stitches, curving the stitches so that the bear has a slight smile.

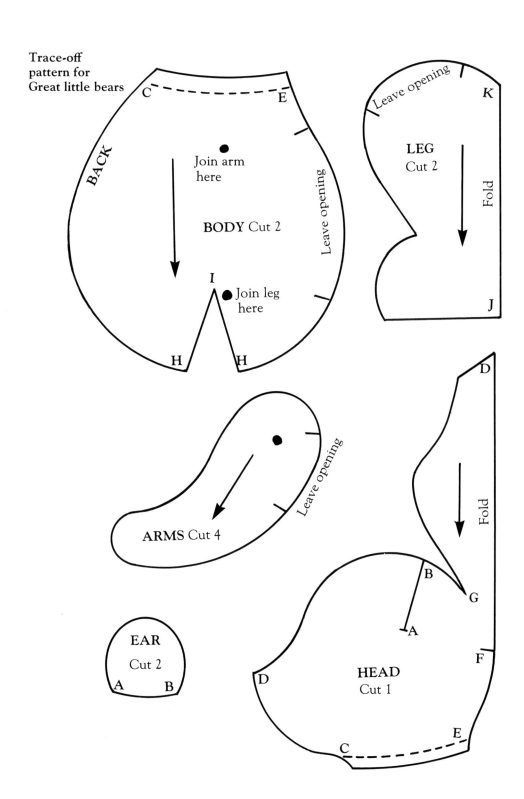

Trace-off pattern for Great little bears

BACK

C E

Join arm here

BODY Cut 2

Leave opening

I

Join leg here

H H

Leave opening

LEG Cut 2

Fold

K

J

ARMS Cut 4

Leave opening

D

Fold

B

A

G

F

EAR Cut 2

A B

HEAD Cut 1

D

C E

31

Mini-bears

You can use these small bears to make toys for babies. Sew several to a cotton cord for a pram toy or hang them from ribbons tied to a lampshade ring to make a nursery mobile.

Materials

Tracing pattern paper
8 × 16in (20 × 40cm) piece of washable, patterned fabric
Washable polyester toy filling
6in (15cm) length of ribbon ¼in (6mm) wide
Stranded embroidery cotton

Preparation

1 Trace the pattern, putting in all the words and marks. Cut out the pattern piece.

2 Cut the fabric into 2 pieces, each 8in (20cm) square. Fold each piece.

3 Pin the pattern to fabric and cut out 2 body pieces on the fold of fabric.

Making the toy

4 Fold the ribbon in two and baste the ends at point A on the right side of one body piece with the loop downwards.

5 Place the second body piece on top, right sides facing. Stitch all round leaving a small opening between the legs.

6 Turn the bear right side out and stuff firmly, then close the opening with ladder stitches.

7 Embroider the eyes and nose in satin stitch and add the mouth in back stitches or stem stitch.

Note: If you want to make the toy from felt, you can join pieces on the wrong side with oversewing.

Trace-off pattern for the Mini-bears

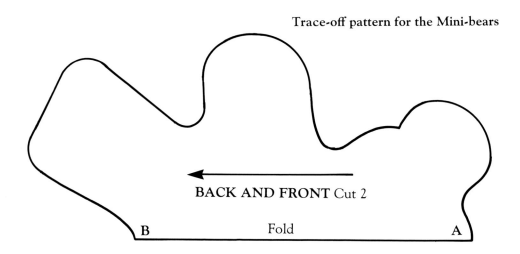

B · BACK AND FRONT Cut 2 · Fold · A

TWO

Traditional Bears

Polar bear

Although real-life polar bears are fearsome animals, toy polar bears are firm favourites with children. This appealing fellow has a shaped head but you should find this quite easy to work.

Materials
Squared pattern paper
20in (50cm) of cream-coloured, curly fur
   fabric 36in (90cm) wide
10in (25cm) square of cream felt
Small safety nose
Pair of black, ¼in (6mm)-diameter safety
   eyes
Washable polyester toy filling

Preparation
1 Draw the graph pattern on squared paper. Put in all the words, numerals and marks. Cut out the pattern pieces.

2 Pin the pattern pieces to the wrong side of the fur fabric, taking note of the directional arrows on the pattern and reversing pieces for left and right sides. From fur fabric, cut out 2 fronts, 1 back on the fold of fabric, 1 back head, 1 front head on the fold of fabric, 2 back arms, and 2 front arms and 2 ears.

3 From felt, cut 2 ears, 2 foot pads and a muzzle.

4 Transfer the pattern markings onto the fabric.

Making the toy
5 Stitch the darts on the front and back head pieces (H – K), leaving ⅛in (3mm) gaps for inserting the eyes on the front piece.

6 Stitch a fur ear to a felt ear, right sides facing, (A – B), along the longest edge. Make two ears. Turn right side out.

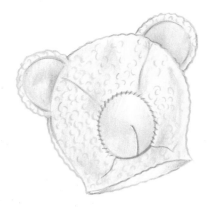

The muzzle is sewn on like this but insert the nose piece first.

7 Baste the ears in position on the front head, felt side downwards.

8 Stitch front and back head pieces together, right sides facing (D – K – K – D). Turn right side out.

9 Stitch the muzzle along edges L – M, leaving a ⅛in (3mm) gap for inserting the nose. Turn right side out.

10 Insert the nose and secure with a washer. Sew the muzzle to the front head using very small, oversewing stitches, leaving a ½in (1cm) gap at the bottom for stuffing. Stuff the muzzle firmly and close the gap with oversewing.

11 Cut the back body piece at E – F to form legs.

Scale: 1 sq = 1in (2.5cm)

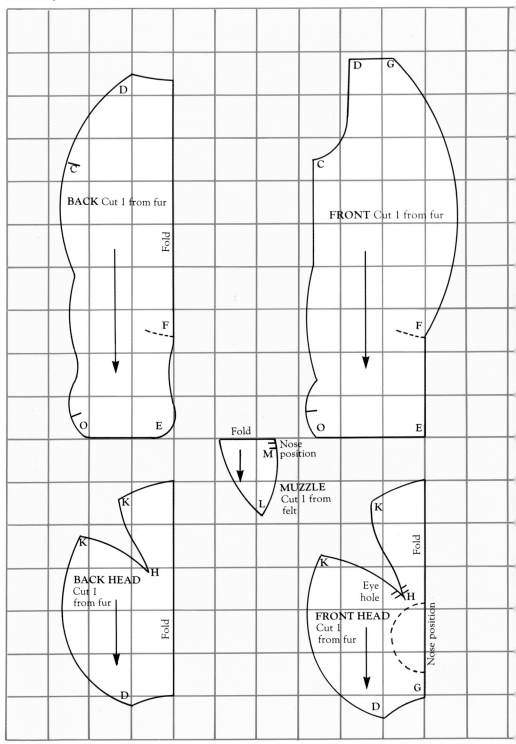

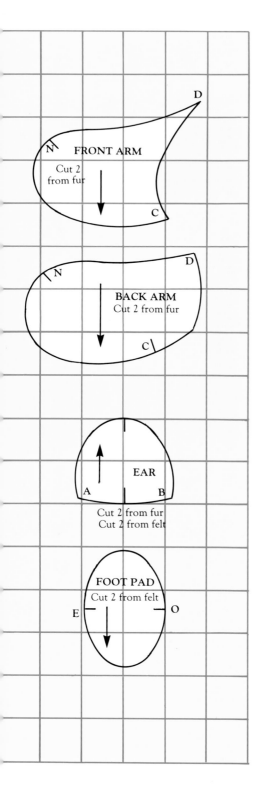

12 Right sides facing, stitch the front arms to the front bodies (C – D). Stitch the back arms to the back body, right sides facing (C – D). Stitch the front bodies together right sides facing (F – G).

13 Stitch the front and back together, right sides facing, along the top of the arms (N – D).

14 Insert the head into the body cavity and, matching points D and G, stitch into position.

15 Stitch the rest of the body together (N – C – O and E – F – E), leaving the bottoms of the legs open for the foot pads and an opening in a side seam for turning.

16 Overstitch the seams at the top of the legs and where the arms join the body.

17 Stitch the felt foot pads into the ends of the legs.

18 Turn the polar bear right side out. Insert the eyes and secure with washers.

19 Stuff the bear firmly. Close the gap with ladder stitches.

Working with fur fabrics
Fur fabrics are available in a wide variety of types, deep pile, shaggy, short pile etc. A lot of different colours and patterns are also available, from pastel shades, browns, beiges, to blacks and greys and some printed with designs to look like animal fur. It is inadvisable to buy fur fabric that is intended for clothing. Safety regulations concerning fabrics for children's toys should always be carefully observed, as some are highly flammable. Suitable fabrics usually have a safety label attached to the fabric bolt.

Baby panda

Pandas are among the world's threatened animal species so this charming toy would make a thoughtful gift for anyone who is interested in wildlife preservation.

Materials
Squared pattern paper
15in (37.5cm) of black fur fabric with a
   short, curly pile 36in (90cm) wide
15in (37.5cm) of white, polished fur
   fabric, 36in (90cm) wide
Pair of ½in (1cm)-diameter safety eyes
Medium-sized safety nose
Black stranded embroidery cotton
Washable polyester toy filling
Wide ribbon for a bow (optional)

Preparation
1 Draw the graph pattern on squared
pattern paper. Put in all words, numerals
and marks. Cut out the pattern pieces.

2 Pin the pattern to the wrong side of the
fur fabrics, taking note of the directional
arrows on the pattern and reversing
pieces for right and left sides.

3 From white fur, cut 1 head piece on
the fold, 2 back pieces, 1 front piece on
the fold and 1 muzzle on the fold.

4 From black fur, cut 4 ear pieces, 1
front arm piece on the fold, 2 back arm
pieces, 1 front leg piece on the fold and 2
back leg pieces. Cut 2 eye patches, adding
¼in (6mm) all round. Transfer the pattern
markings onto the fabric.

Making the toy
5 Stitch the gusset into the head piece,
right sides facing (A – B).

6 Stitch the dart C – D at the back of the
head, right sides facing.

7 Pierce holes for the eyes on the head
piece in the positions marked.

8 Stitch the muzzle to the head, right
sides facing (G – B – E – B – G).

9 Stitch the muzzle F – G – H, right sides
facing, leaving a ⅛in (3mm) gap for
inserting the nose peg. Turn the head
right side out.

10 Pierce small holes in the eye patches
(see pattern for position). Turn the patch
edges under ¼in (6mm) and sew to the
head using very small stitches.

11 Insert the eyes through the holes in
both patch and head piece and secure
with washers. Insert the toy nose in the
same way.

12 Stitch the back legs to the back body
pieces, right sides facing (I – J). Stitch the
back arms to the back bodies (K – D).

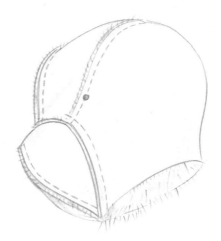

Stitch the gusset on the head piece and then
stitch in the muzzle.

40

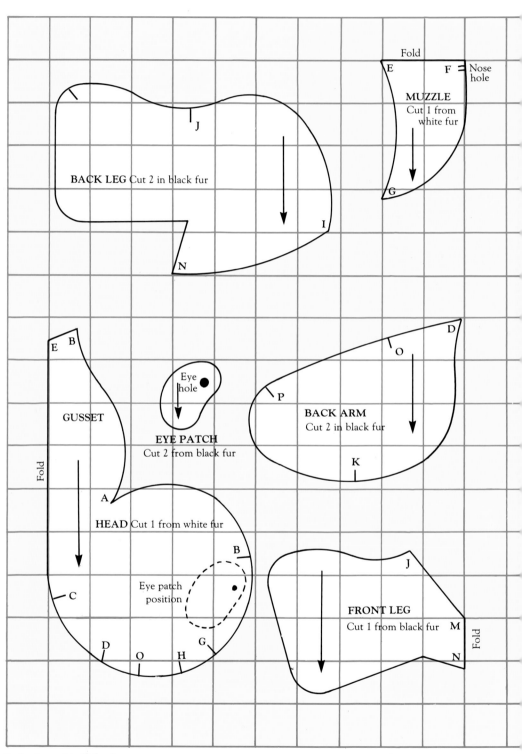

BACK LEG Cut 2 in black fur

Fold

E   F   Nose hole

MUZZLE
Cut 1 from white fur

G

J

I

N

E   B

GUSSET

Fold

Eye hole

EYE PATCH
Cut 2 from black fur

D

O

P

BACK ARM
Cut 2 in black fur

K

A

HEAD Cut 1 from white fur

B

Eye patch
position

C

D

O   H   G

J

FRONT LEG
Cut 1 from black fur   M

Fold

N

Scale: 1 sq = 1in (2.5cm)

42

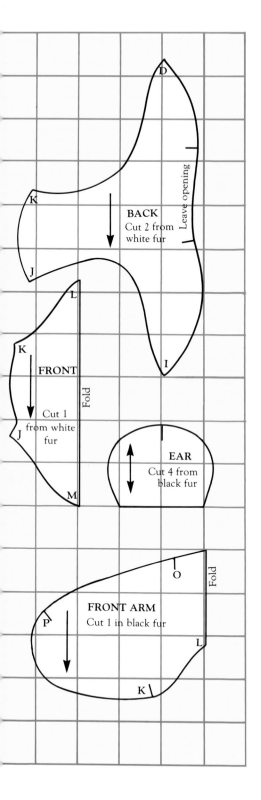

BACK
Cut 2 from white fur

Leave opening

FRONT
Cut 1 from white fur

Fold

EAR
Cut 4 from black fur

FRONT ARM
Cut 1 in black fur

Fold

13 Stitch the front arms to the front body, right sides facing (K – L). Stitch the front legs to the front body (J – M).

14 Stitch the back body pieces together, right sides facing (D – I – N), leaving a gap in a seam for turning.

15 Snip into the curved seams for ease.

16 Stitch the body pieces together, right sides facing, from O – P, along the top of the arms.

17 Insert and baste the head into the body cavity, matching the head and body pieces at O and D. Stitch in place.

18 Stitch the body pieces together (P – K – J – N – J – K – P).

19 Turn the toy right side out. Stuff solidly so that there is no feeling of 'squashiness'. Close the seam with ladder stitches.

20 Stitch the ear pieces together in pairs along the curved, notched edges. Turn right side out. Turn a ¼in (6mm) hem on the lower edges and oversew. Sew the ears to the top of the panda's head. The position of the ears is important. Study the picture and pin, then baste, the ears in a pleasing position before sewing.

21 Using 3 strands of embroidery cotton, work a smile under the nose in stem stitch.

Sew a panda
The panda is one of the rarest animals in the world although conservation programmes are increasing the animal's numbers. This simple pattern could be made up into toys for fund-raising events but designs in books, like this one, are copyright and cannot be sold for personal profit.

43

Chubby bear

Chubby is a big, cuddly bear, so squashy and comforting that he'll become a much-loved friend in no time at all. Take special care with the positioning of the eyes.

Materials
Squared pattern paper
48in (135cm) of cream-coloured, closely-woven fur fabric, 36in (90cm) wide
12in (30cm) square of cream-coloured felt
Pair of $\frac{3}{4}$in (18mm)-diameter safety eyes
Medium-sized safety nose
Washable polyester toy filling
Black stranded embroidery cotton

Preparation
1 Draw the graph pattern on squared paper. Put in all words, numerals and marks. Cut out the pattern pieces.

2 Pin the pattern pieces to the wrong side of the fur fabric, taking note of the directional arrows on the pattern and reversing pieces for right and left sides. From fur fabric, cut 1 front body and arm on the fold, 2 back bodies, 2 front legs, 1 head gusset on the fold, 2 side heads and 2 ear pieces. From felt, cut 2 ear pieces and 2 foot pads. Transfer the pattern marks onto the fabrics.

Making the toy
3 Right sides facing, stitch each fur ear to a felt ear (A – B) along the curved, notched edge. Turn right side out.

4 Baste the ears in the slits in the side head pieces (A – X). Turn the ears forwards, towards the nose and baste along X – B. Stitch along A – X. (Make sure that the felt side of the ears faces towards the nose.)

5 Stitch the side head pieces together (C – D), leaving a $\frac{1}{8}$in (3mm) gap at D for the nose peg (see pattern).

6 Baste the head gusset between the side heads (E – D – E) and stitch in place, leaving $\frac{1}{8}$in (3mm) gaps for the eye pegs.

7 Stitch the neck darts in the side head pieces.

8 Insert the safety eyes and nose through the gaps and secure with washers. Turn the head right side out.

9 Stitch the front legs to the front body (F – G). Stitch the front legs together (G – H).

10 Baste the front body to the back body pieces (H – I and J – F – K) around the limbs leaving I – J open to insert the felt foot pads. (The fabric will need to be eased into place at F where the arms and legs meet.) Stitch H – I and J – F – K.

11 Stitch the foot pads in place (I – J – I).

12 Stitch the arms darts.

13 Stitch the back body pieces together (E – L).

14 Insert and baste the head in the body cavity, right sides facing, and matching C and E, then stitch.

15 Stitch the darts in the back body pieces.

16 Stitch the back body pieces together (M – H). Turn right side out through L – M.

17 Stuff the bear so that it feels comfortably 'squashy'. Insert the stuffing in small amounts, teasing it out so that it is bulky and airy. Close the seam with ladder stitches.

18 Trim the fur pile from around the muzzle. Mark the mouth with chalk pencil then embroider it, using 2 strands of embroidery cotton, working in stem stitch (see picture).

45

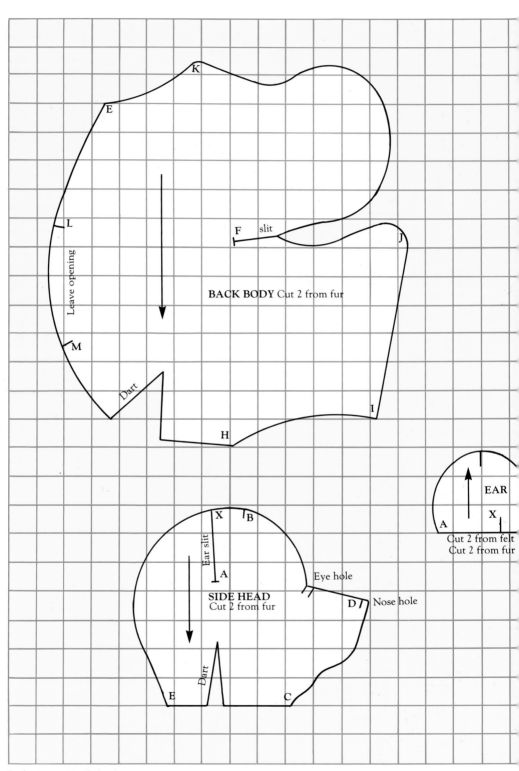

K

E

L

Leave opening

F   slit

J

BACK BODY Cut 2 from fur

M

Dart

I

H

EAR

A   X

Cut 2 from felt
Cut 2 from fur

X   B

Ear slit

A

SIDE HEAD
Cut 2 from fur

Eye hole

D   Nose hole

Dart

E   C

Scale: 1 sq = 1in (2.5cm)

46

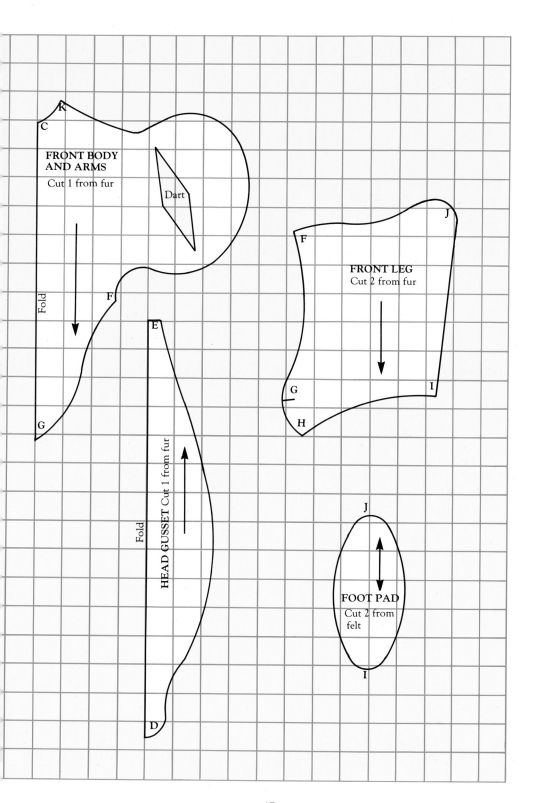

**FRONT BODY
AND ARMS**

Cut 1 from fur

Dart

Fold

FRONT LEG
Cut 2 from fur

HEAD GUSSET Cut 1 from fur

Fold

FOOT PAD

Cut 2 from
felt

47

Feeling blue?

A chubby and very appealing bear who is guaranteed to cheer everyone up in no time at all. The silky fur fabric pelt and a softly-stuffed body, makes this a very cuddly toy.

Materials
Squared pattern paper
30in (75cm) of blue, polished fur fabric
  36in (90cm) wide
12in (30cm) square of matching blue felt
Pair of ⅜in (9mm)-diameter safety eyes
Small safety nose
Washable polyester toy filling

Preparation
1 Draw the graph pattern on squared pattern paper. Put in all the words, numerals and marks. Cut out the pattern pieces.

2 Pin the pattern pieces to the wrong side of the fur fabric, taking note of the directional arrows and reversing pieces for left and right sides. Cut out 1 back head, 1 forehead, 2 front heads and 2 ear pieces. On the fold of fabric, cut 1 body piece, 1 back body and 1 base.

3 From felt, cut 2 foot pads, 2 ear pieces and 1 muzzle on the fold of fabric.

Making the toy
4 Stitch the forehead to the front head pieces (A – B).

5 Stitch each fur ear to a felt ear along the curved, notched edge (E – F). Turn the ears right side out.

6 Baste the ears in position on the right side of the back head piece with the felt side facing upwards.

7 Stitch the muzzle to the front head piece matching points C and G.

8 Stitch the muzzle and face pieces together, right sides facing (D – C – H), leaving a ⅛in (3mm) gap at H for inserting the nose peg.

9 Stitch the front and back heads together, right sides facing (I – B – B – I).

10 Pierce small holes for the eyes (see pattern) and insert the eyes and nose, reinforcing the surrounding fabric with running stitches. Secure with washers.

11 Stitch the neck dart in the back head piece. Turn the bear right side out.

12 Stitch the base piece to the back body, right sides facing (J – K – J). Cut the front body piece and base for legs (see pattern).

13 Right sides facing, stitch the front body to the back body around the limbs on each side I – L and M – N – M to form legs, and leaving a gap in a seam for turning and stuffing. (L – M is left open for putting in the foot pads.)

14 Stitch the darts on the arms and feet on the front body piece. Stitch the foot pads in place (L – M – O – L).

15 Insert and baste the head into the body, right sides facing and matching points I and D at the front. Stitch in place.

16 Turn the bear right side out and stuff so that it feels 'squashy'. Close the opening with ladder stitches.

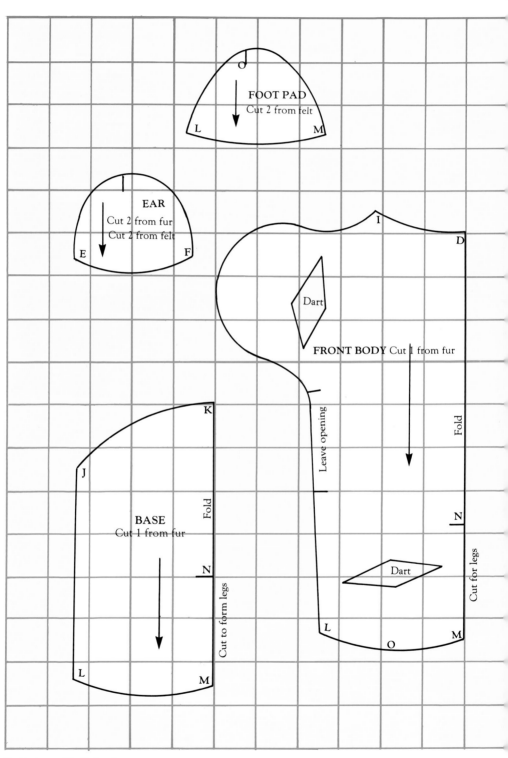

FOOT PAD
Cut 2 from felt

EAR
Cut 2 from fur
Cut 2 from felt

FRONT BODY Cut 1 from fur

Dart

Leave opening

Fold

Fold

Cut for legs

N

N

D

I

E   F

J   K

Dart

L   M   O

BASE
Cut 1 from fur

Cut to form legs

L   M

Scale: 1 sq = 1in (2.5cm)

50

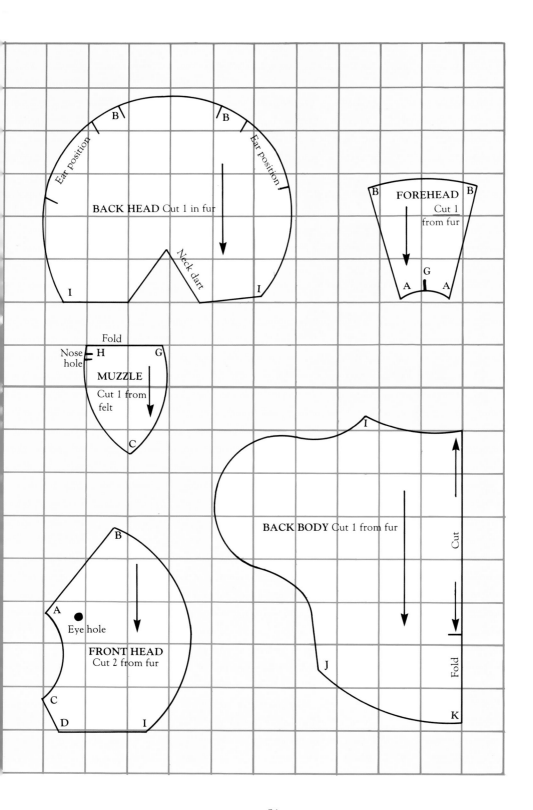

BACK HEAD Cut 1 in fur

B   B
Ear position   Ear position
Neck dart
I   I

FOREHEAD
Cut 1
from fur
B   B
A   G   A

Fold
Nose
hole   H   G
MUZZLE
Cut 1 from
felt
C

BACK BODY Cut 1 from fur
I
Cut
J
Fold
K

B
A
Eye hole
FRONT HEAD
Cut 2 from fur
C
D   I

51

Edwardian bear

This is one of the most popular of all bears, with authentic-looking details, such as the head shape, the embroidered muzzle, long arms and jointed limbs. The bear stands about 13in (32.5cm) tall.

Materials
Squared pattern paper
40in (100cm) of gold-coloured fur fabric
  36in (90cm) wide
10in (25cm) square of light-brown felt
Pair of ⅜in (9mm)-diameter safety eyes
4 sets of 1¾in (4.5cm)-diameter plastic
  joints
1 set of 1¼in (4.5cm)-diameter plastic
  joints
Washable polyester toy filling
Brown stranded embroidery cotton

Preparation
1 Draw the graph pattern on squared
pattern paper. Put in all words, numerals
and marks. Cut out the pattern pieces.

2 Pin the patterns to the wrong side of
the fur fabric, taking note of the
directional arrows and reversing pieces
for right and left sides.

3 From fur fabric, cut 2 front pieces,
2 back pieces, 2 leg pieces on the fold,
2 inner arms, 2 outer arms, 2 head pieces,
1 head gusset on the fold and 2 ear
pieces. From felt, cut 2 ear pieces, 2 paws
and 2 foot pads. Transfer the pattern
marks onto the fabric.

Making the toy
4 Stitch each fur ear to a felt ear, right
sides facing, along the curved, notched
edge (A – B). Turn right side out.

5 Stitch the darts in the head pieces,
inserting the ears at A and making sure
that the felt sides face forwards. Baste the
ears in place (A – X). Turn the ears
forward towards the nose and baste
(X – B). Stitch the ears in place (A – X).

6 Stitch the head pieces together (C – D).

7 Baste the head gusset between the head
pieces, matching D and E. Stitch, leaving
⅛in (3mm) gaps for the eye pegs (see
pattern). Turn right side out.

8 Stitch the paws to the inner arms, right
sides facing (F – G).

9 Pierce holes in the fabric for the arm
pegs, as indicated on the pattern. Stitch
the outer and inner arms pieces together,
right sides facing, leaving part of the seam
open for turning. (Make sure the opening
is large enough to insert the joint.) Turn
the arms right sides out.

10 Insert the peg of the arm joint
through the pierced hole from the inside
of the arm. Work both arms in the same
way. Stuff the arms firmly and then close
the open seam with ladder stitches.

11 Stitch the leg seams (H – I), leaving
the same size gap in the seams (as you did
for the arms) for turning. Insert the felt
foot pads in the bottom of the legs, right
sides facing, baste and stitch (J – I – J).

12 Pierce a hole for the leg pegs in the
position marked on the leg pattern.
(Make sure you have a right leg and a left
leg.) Turn the legs right side out. Insert
the peg of the joint through the hole
from inside the leg. Stuff the legs firmly
and ladder-stitch the open seam.

13 Stitch the left front piece and the left
back piece together, right sides facing (K
– L – M), leaving ⅛in (3mm) gaps for
inserting the leg and arm pegs.

14 Stitch the right front and right back in the same way.

15 Stitch the two sides of the bear together, right sides facing (K – N – M – K), leaving a $\frac{1}{4}$in (6mm) opening at K to insert the head peg and an opening in the back for stuffing.

16 Turn the body right side out. Insert the eyes in the head and secure with the

washers. Stuff the head very firmly. When the head is as full as possible, insert the head peg.

17 Using strong thread and running stitches, gather the edges of the head (C – E – C) around the peg. Fasten off.

18 Insert the peg into the body at K and secure from inside the body with disc and washer.

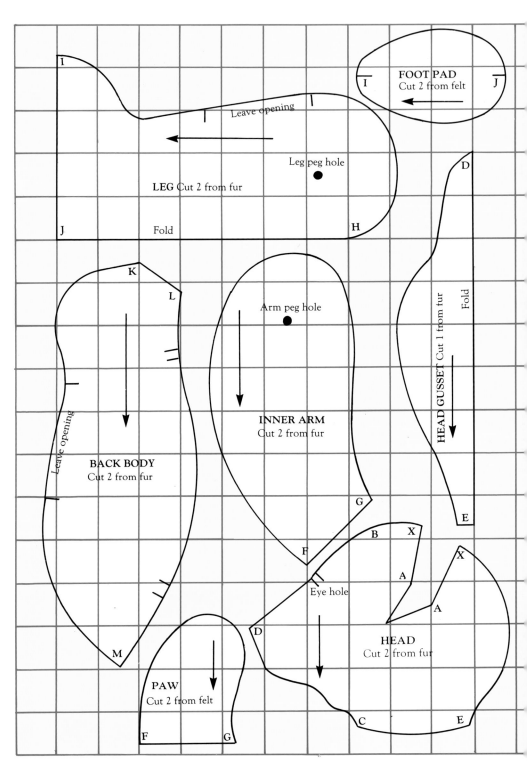

Scale: 1 sq = 1in (2.5cm)

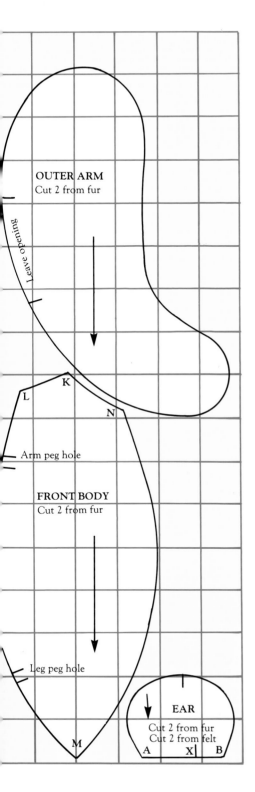

OUTER ARM
Cut 2 from fur

Leave opening

K

L

N

Arm peg hole

FRONT BODY
Cut 2 from fur

Leg peg hole

M

EAR

Cut 2 from fur
Cut 2 from felt

A   X   B

Gather the edges of the head round the head peg.

19 Insert the arm pegs and leg pegs into the body at the points marked (making sure the limbs are facing the right way) and secure from inside the body. (It is important that the legs and arms are the right way round because once the discs and washers are secured they cannot be removed.)

20 Stuff the body very firmly. Close the open seam with ladder stitches.

21 Trim the fur pile away from around the muzzle. Using 6 strands of embroidery cotton, embroider a nose and a mouth.

Work satin stitches, first down the nose, then across.

55

THREE

All Dressed Up

Poppet bear

Most bears are males. This one is undoubtedly a female bear, with a very cute expression on her face. You can choose any colour of fur fabric for her pelt, with a matching felt tummy.

Materials
Squared pattern paper
30in (75cm) of toffee-coloured fur fabric
  36in (90cm) wide
10in (25cm) square of matching felt
Scrap of black felt
Pair of ⅝in (15mm)-diameter safety eyes
Black stranded embroidery cotton
Washable polyester toy filling
Ribbon for a hair bow (optional)

Preparation
1 Draw the graph pattern on squared pattern paper. Put in all words, numerals and marks. Cut out the pattern pieces.

2 Pin the paper pattern to the wrong side of the fur fabric, taking note of the directional arrows and reversing pieces for left and right sides.

3 From fur fabric, cut out 2 back pieces, 2 front arm pieces, 2 front legs, 2 ear pieces, 1 head gusset on the fold of fabric, 2 side head pieces. From the toffee-coloured felt, cut 1 front body on the fold of fabric, 2 ear pieces and 2 paws. From black felt cut 1 nose piece. Cut the slits A – X in the head pieces.

Making the toy
4 Stitch each fur ear to a felt ear, right sides facing, along the curved, notched edge (A – B). Turn the ears right sides out.

5 Baste the ears in the slits on the right side of the head pieces (A – X). Turn the remainder of the ear to the front of the head and baste X – B. Stitch along A – X.

6 Stitch the side head pieces together, right sides facing, C – D.

7 Baste the head gusset between the side head pieces, right sides facing (E – D – E). Stitch. Pierce small holes in the positions marked (see pattern). Insert the safety eyes and reinforce the fabric by working running stitches around the peg. Secure with washers. Turn right side out.

8 Sew the nose along F – G, using oversewing. Turn right side out.

9 Matching G to the point D on the head, pin the nose in place and then oversew round the edges.

Sew the nose F – G then oversew to the face.

10 Stitch the paws to the front arms (H – I), right sides facing. Stitch the front arms to the front body, right sides facing (J – K).

11 Stitch the front legs to the front body, right sides facing (K – M). Stitch the front legs together M – N. Snip the back body piece to the point K (see pattern).

12 Stitch the front body to the back pieces along the limbs (N – O – K – L).

13 Insert the head piece into the body cavity, right sides facing and matching points C – J and E – P. Stitch the neck seam.

14 Stitch the darts in the back pieces (Q – R).

15 Stitch the back of the bear along P – Q – N, leaving a gap in the seam for stuffing. Turn right side out.

16 Stuff the head firmly. Stuff the body less firmly. Close the open seams with ladder stitches.

17 Embroider the mouth in back stitches (refer to the picture).

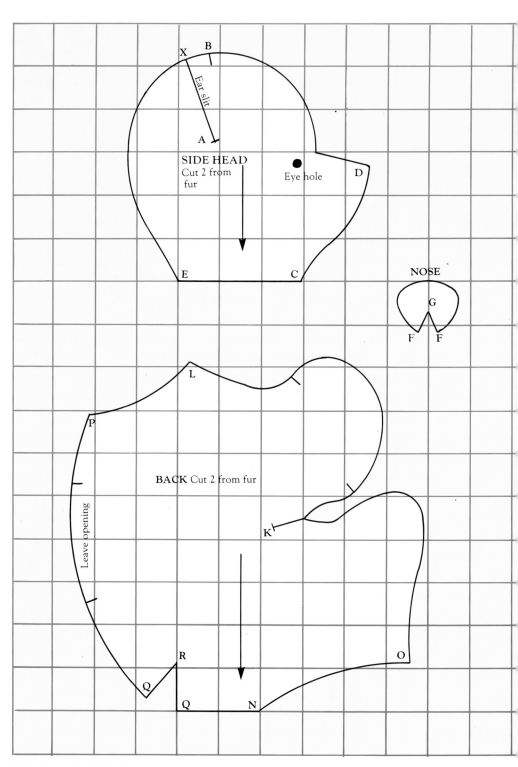

X B

Ear slit

A

SIDE HEAD
Cut 2 from
fur

Eye hole

D

E C

NOSE

G

F F

L

P

BACK Cut 2 from fur

Leave opening

K

R

O

Q

Q N

Scale: 1 sq = 1in (2.5cm)

60

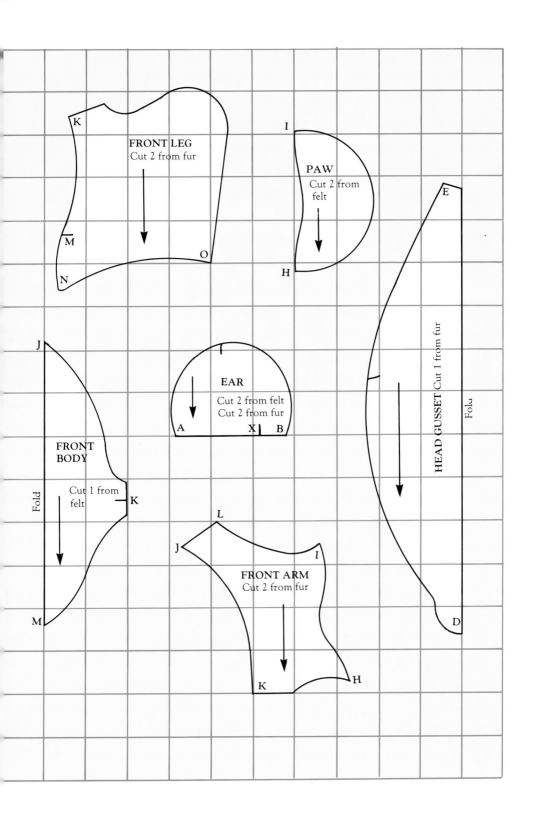

FRONT LEG
Cut 2 from fur

K

M

N

O

PAW
Cut 2 from felt

I

H

EAR
Cut 2 from felt
Cut 2 from fur

A   X   B

HEAD GUSSET Cut 1 from fur

E

Fold

D

FRONT BODY

Cut 1 from felt

K

J

M

Fold

FRONT ARM
Cut 2 from fur

L

J   I

K   H

Country bear

This cute little fellow in a country-style waistcoat stands up on his flat-bottomed feet – but he is still very cuddly. Ideal for a child this bear would be equally loved by an adult bear collector.

Materials

Squared pattern paper
20in (50cm) of cream-coloured fur fabric, 36in (90cm) wide
10in (25cm) square of beige felt
Washable polyester toy filling
Pair of ⅜in (10mm)-diameter amber-coloured safety eyes
Dark brown stranded embroidery cotton
12in (30cm) square of blue felt

Preparation

1 Draw the graph pattern on squared paper. Put in all words, numerals and marks. Cut out the pattern pieces.

2 Pin the pattern pieces to the wrong side of the fur fabric, taking note of the directional arrows on the pattern and reversing pieces for right and left sides. Cut out 2 heads, 2 body pieces on the fold of fabric, 2 fabric ears and 1 gusset. Cut 2 foot pads and 2 ears from felt. Transfer the pattern markings onto the fabric.

Making the toy

3 Stitch the darts in both head pieces.

4 Stitch the head pieces together (A – B). Stitch the head gusset between the head pieces, right sides facing, stitching from C, through B and back to C, leaving ⅛in (3mm) holes in the seam where indicated on the pattern for inserting the the eyes. Turn right side out.

5 Stitch the body pieces together (G – F) along the top of the arms.

6 Insert and baste the head into the body cavity, right sides facing, matching points

Leave ½in (1cm) of the head protruding above the neck and run a gathering thread round.

A and C and with ½in (1cm) of the head protruding above the body neckline. Make sure that the front head faces the same way as the body front. Stitch the head to the body.

7 Run a gathering thread round the protruding head edge, leaving long thread ends hanging outside the body.

8 Make up two pairs of ears, fabric to felt, right sides facing (D – E), leaving the straight edge open. Turn right side out and, turning in a ¼in (6mm) hem, oversew the straight edges.

9 Cut the front and back body pieces along I – J to form legs.

10 Stitch the body pieces together (G – H and I – J – I), leaving H – I – H open for inserting the foot pads. Leave a gap in the seam for turning. Over-stitch the seams by ½in (1cm) at the points where the body joins the arms and between the legs.

11 Insert the felt foot pads, right sides facing, and stitch or oversew in place. Insert the safety eyes in the positions marked on the pattern.

12 Turn the bear right side out and stuff the head firmly. Pull up the gathering threads at the neck and fasten off the thread ends. Stuff the rest of the bear less firmly so that it has a 'squashy' feel. Close the opening with ladder stitches.

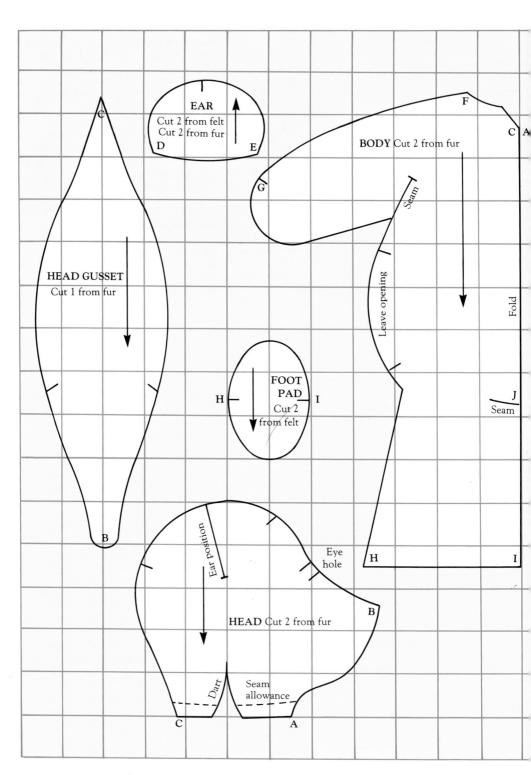

EAR
Cut 2 from felt
Cut 2 from fur

D   E

BODY Cut 2 from fur

F

C A

G

Seam

Leave opening

Fold

HEAD GUSSET
Cut 1 from fur

FOOT
PAD
Cut 2
from felt

H   I

J
Seam

H   I

B

Ear Position

Eye
hole

B

HEAD Cut 2 from fur

Dart

Seam
allowance

C   A

Scale: 1 sq = 1in (2.5cm)

64

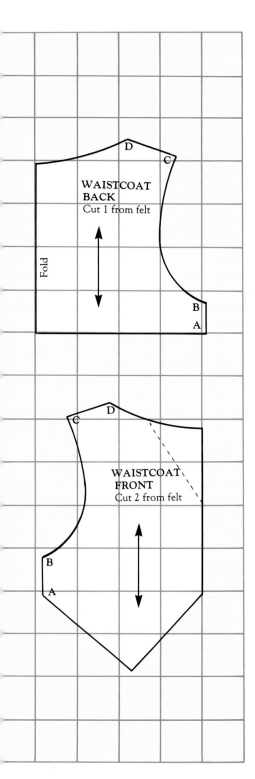

WAISTCOAT
BACK
Cut 1 from felt

Fold

D
C
B
A

C
D
WAISTCOAT
FRONT
Cut 2 from felt

B
A

Ladder-stitch the ears to the head.

13 Sew the ears to the head in the positions marked on the pattern, using ladder stitches.

14 Embroider the nose and mouth, using 3 strands of embroidery cotton.

WAISTCOAT
15 Draw the pattern for the waistcoat on squared paper. Cut out and pin the pieces to the blue felt. Cut out 1 back on the fold and 2 fronts.

16 Oversew the shoulder and side seams together.

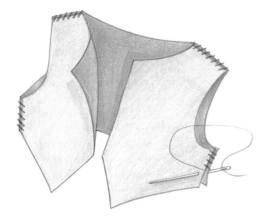

Oversew the side seams and shoulder seams.

Great-uncle Humphrey

He's a serious bear and a bit of a bookworm but quite lovable. Humphrey would make an ideal friend for an older child – or even an adult.

Materials
Squared pattern paper
48in (135cm) of black, close-curled fur, 36in (90cm) wide
10in (25cm) square of black felt
Pair of black, $\frac{3}{8}$in (9mm)-diameter safety eyes
1 large safety nose
Washable polyester toy filling

Preparation
1 Draw the graph pattern on squared paper, putting in all the words, numerals and marks. Cut out the pattern pieces and pin the pattern to the wrong side of the fur fabric, taking note of the directional arrows and reversing pieces for right and left sides.

2 From fur fabric cut out 2 back body pieces, 1 head gusset on the fold, 2 front arms and 2 front legs, reversing the pattern for left and right. Cut 1 front body on the fold, and 2 ear pieces. From felt, cut 2 ear pieces and 1 muzzle on the fold. Transfer the pattern markings onto the fabric.

Making the toy
3 Stitch each fur ear to a felt ear, right sides facing, (A – B), along the curved, notched edge. Turn the ears right side out.

4 Baste the ears in position on the right side of the back body pieces, in the slits on the head pieces (A – X – B), turning X – B on the ears forwards towards the front of the head. Stitch along Y – A – X. The felt side of the ears should face forwards, to the front of the head.

5 Stitch the front legs to the front body (E – F).

6 Stitch the front arms to the front body (G – F).

7 Stitch the darts in the back body pieces, Stitch the back body pieces together (H – I).

8 Stitch the front body to the back body around the limbs (H – E – F – G – J), for both sides.

9 Stitch the head gusset in position (C – D) leaving $\frac{1}{8}$in (3mm) gaps as indicated on the pattern.

10 Stitch the muzzle in position matching points L and J on the head.

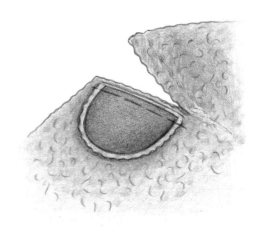

Baste the made-up ear into the head slit.

11 Stitch the front of the bear
(M – J – K) leaving a $\frac{1}{8}$in (3mm) hole for
the nose peg at M.

12 Stitch the back of the bear (N – D – I)
leaving an opening (see pattern) for
turning and stuffing.

13 Turn the bear right side out. Stuff the
head, upper body cavity, arms and legs
firmly and to shape. Stuff the lower body
cavity so that it is less firm and a bit
'squashy'. Close the opening in the back
of the bear with ladder stitches.

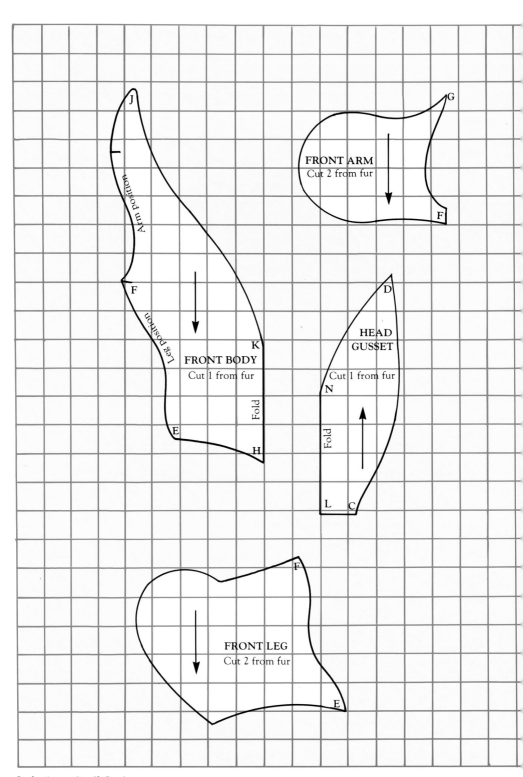

Scale: 1 sq = 1in (2.5cm)

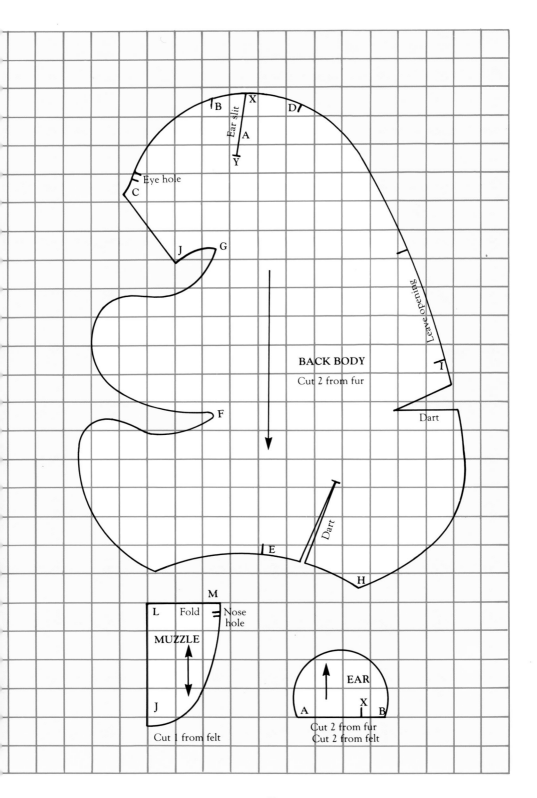

B
X
D
Ear slit
A
Y
Eye hole
C
J
G
F

BACK BODY

Cut 2 from fur

Leave opening

I

Dart

Dart

E
H

M
L Fold Nose hole

MUZZLE

J

Cut 1 from felt

EAR

A X B

Cut 2 from fur
Cut 2 from felt

FOUR

Special Bears

Kate Koala

Here is the Australian teddy bear – the koala. Koalas have a distinctive flat nose and, in Australia, live in the top branches of the eucalyptus tree. Sitting, this bear is 8in (20cm) high.

Materials
Squared pattern paper
10in (25cm) square of white, short-pile fur fabric
10in (25cm) square of brown, long-pile fur fabric
20in (50cm) of mushroom-coloured wool fabric 36in (90cm) wide
10in (25cm) square of black felt
Scrap of red felt
Pair of ¾in (18mm)-diameter safety eyes
Washable polyester toy filling

Preparation
1 Draw the graph pattern on squared pattern paper. Put in all the words, numerals and marks, Cut out the pattern pieces.

2 Pin the pattern pieces to the wrong side of the fur fabrics, taking note of the directional arrows. Pin the pattern pieces to the wool fabric. Reverse pieces as required for right and left sides.

3 From white fur fabric, cut 1 front body piece on the fold. From the brown fur fabric, cut 2 ear pieces. From wool fabric, cut 2 back body pieces, 2 front arms, 2 inside paws, 2 front legs, 2 side head pieces, 2 ear pieces and 1 head gusset on the fold. From black felt, cut 2 nose pieces. From red felt, cut 1 tongue. Transfer all the patterns marks onto the fabrics.

Making the toy
4 Right sides facing, stitch each wool ear to a fur ear along the curved, notched edge (A – B). Turn the ears right side out.

5 Baste the ears into the slits on the right side of the side head pieces (A – X), basting the remainder of the ear (X – B) along the head piece. (The wool side of the ears must face the front of the head.) Stitch A – X.

6 Stitch the head pieces together along the muzzle (C – D).

7 Baste the head gusset between the head pieces (E – D – E). Stitch.

8 Stitch the darts in the side head pieces (G – H). Pierce the eye holes in the head pieces (see pattern). Insert the eyes and secure with the washers. Turn the head right side out.

9 Stitch the felt nose pieces together along the notched side (I – J). Turn the nose right side out.

10 Stitch the nose to the head using small oversewing stitches and leaving an opening at the base for stuffing. Lightly stuff the nose and close the opening with oversewing.

11 Stitch the front paws to the front arms, right sides facing (K – L). Stitch the front arms to the front body, right sides facing, (M – N).

12 Stitch the front legs to the front body, right sides facing (N – O). Stitch the front legs together (O – P).

13 Make a cut in the back body piece from the point where the arms and legs join to N (see pattern).

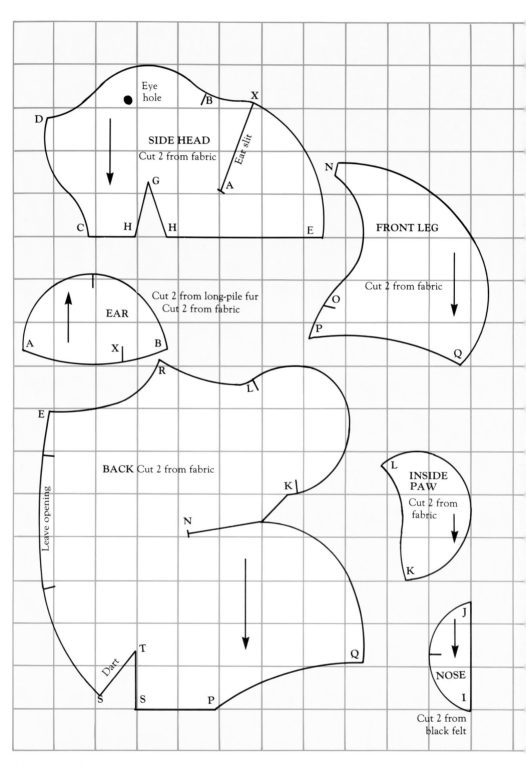

Eye hole

SIDE HEAD
Cut 2 from fabric

Ear slit

B

X

D

A

G

C   H   H

E

FRONT LEG

N

Cut 2 from fabric

O

P

Q

EAR

Cut 2 from long-pile fur
Cut 2 from fabric

A

X

B

R

L

E

BACK Cut 2 from fabric

Leave opening

K

N

INSIDE PAW

Cut 2 from fabric

L

K

Dart

T

S   S   P

Q

J

NOSE

I

Cut 2 from black felt

Scale: 1 sq = 1in (2.5cm)

74

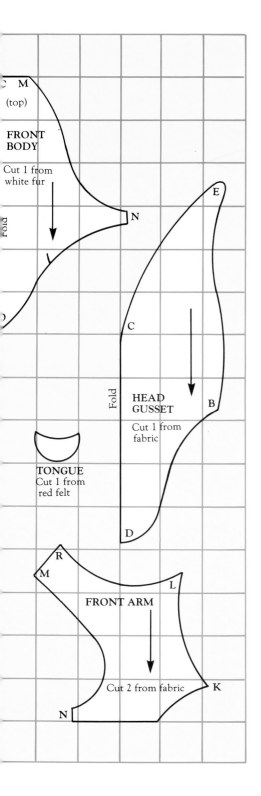

FRONT BODY
Cut 1 from white fur

C M
(top)

Fold

N

E

C

Fold

HEAD GUSSET
Cut 1 from fabric

B

TONGUE
Cut 1 from red felt

D

R

M

L

FRONT ARM

Cut 2 from fabric

K

N

14 Stitch the back body pieces to the front body along the limbs (P – Q – N – K – L – R).

15 Stitch the darts in the back body pieces (S – T).

16 Stitch the head to the body matching at points E – C – E.

17 Stitch the backs together from the top of the head gusset to the base (U – P) leaving an opening for turning. Turn right side out.

18 Position the tongue and oversew in place about ¼in (6mm) below the muzzle seam (see picture).

19 Stuff the head and body firmly and close the open seam with ladder stitches.

Paws and claws
Claws can be a charming finishing touch on a bear's paws, especially if the bear is softly stuffed. Work the claws in chain stitches, using tapisserie wool or soft embroidery cotton. Remember that bears have only four claws. The embroidery can be worked before or after the limbs are made up.

Safe fillings
Always use the best toy filling you can afford – Dacron and polyester are both very good. Do not use foam chips for filling toys as they are dangerous to children. It is advisable to use only those toy fillings that are stated to meet the current safety standards.

Velvety bear

As any child will tell you, toy bears do not have to be brown, grey or black – they can be any colour at all. This little chubby bear is made of blue cotton velvet.

Materials
Squared pattern paper
20in (50cm) of velvet fabric 36in (90cm) wide
Pair of ⅜in (9mm)-diameter safety eyes
1 small safety nose
Washable polyester toy filling

Preparation
1 Draw the graph pattern on squared paper. Put in all words, numerals and marks. Cut out the pattern pieces.

2 Pin the patterns to the wrong side of the fabric, taking note of the directional arrows, and reversing pieces for right and left sides. Cut out 2 side head pieces, 1 head gusset on the fold, 2 nose pieces, 4 ear pieces, 2 back legs, 2 back arms, 2 front legs, 2 front arms, 2 foot pads, 2 front body pieces and 1 back body piece on the fold. Transfer the pattern marks onto the fabric.

Making the toy
3 Stitch the ears together in pairs, right sides facing, along the curved, notched side (A – B). Turn the ears to the right side.

4 Baste the ears in the slits on the right side of the head pieces. Stitch along (A – B).

5 Baste the head gusset between the head pieces (C – D), leaving ⅛in (3mm) gaps in the seam for the eye pegs (see pattern).

6 Stitch the nose pieces together (E – G).

7 Stitch the nose to the head (F – E – F). Stitch up the muzzle (F – G) leaving a ⅛in

(3mm) gap in the seam at G for the nose peg. Turn right side out.

8 Insert the eyes and nose and secure with washers.

9 Stitch the front arms to the front body pieces, right sides facing (H – I).

10 Stitch the front legs to the front body pieces, right sides facing (J – K). Stitch the front body pieces together, right sides facing (L – M).

11 Stitch the back arms to the back body piece, right sides facing (H – I), then stitch the back legs to the back body piece (J – K).

12 Stitch the front and back together along the top of the arms (X – H), leaving a hole for the head.

13 Insert the head, right sides facing, and baste in place, matching points F and M, thus making sure that the head is facing the right way round. Stitch.

14 Stitch the rest of the front and back bodies together (X – I – J – N and O – P), leaving N – O open for inserting the foot pads.

15 Stitch the foot pads in place (N – O – N).

16 Turn the bear right side out through the opening in the base and stuff very fully, taking special care with the head. Close the seam with ladder stitches.

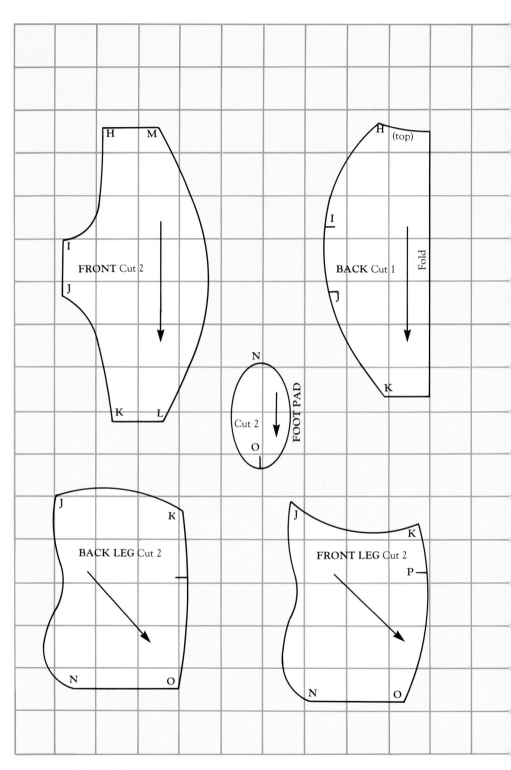

Scale: 1 sq = 1in (2.5cm)

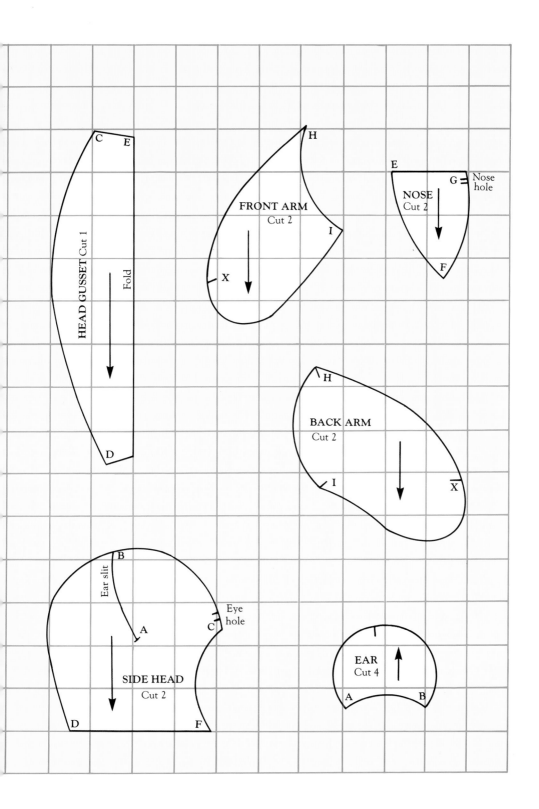

C E

HEAD GUSSET Cut 1

Fold

D

H

FRONT ARM
Cut 2

X

I

E

NOSE
Cut 2

G Nose hole

F

H

BACK ARM
Cut 2

I

X

B

Ear slit

A

C Eye hole

SIDE HEAD
Cut 2

D

F

EAR
Cut 4

A

B

Sweetheart bear

This little cutie says all the right things like 'I love you' and 'I'm thinking of you'. Embroider words or just initials on the heart but work the embroidery before sewing the heart in place.

Materials
Squared pattern paper
Tracing paper
24in (60cm) of white, polished fur 36in (90cm) wide
10in (25cm) square of red felt
Pair of $\frac{3}{8}$in (9mm)-diameter safety eyes
Small safety nose
Washable polyester toy filling

Preparation
1 Draw the graph pattern on squared paper. Put in all the words, numerals and marks. Cut out the pattern pieces. Trace the heart pattern on folded tracing paper.

2 Pin the patterns to the wrong side of the fur fabric taking note of the directional arrows and reversing pieces for right and left sides. Cut 2 side head pieces, 1 head gusset on the fold, 4 ear pieces, 2 back arm pieces, 1 back body on the fold and 1 front body on the fold. Transfer the pattern markings onto the fabric. Pin the heart pattern to folded red felt and cut out.

Making the toy
3 Stitch the ears together in pairs, right sides facing, along the curved, notched edge (A – B). Turn the ears right side out.

4 Baste the ears into the slits on the right side of the head pieces (A – X – B). Stitch the ears in place (A – X).

5 Stitch the side head pieces together, right sides facing, (C – D), leaving a $\frac{1}{8}$in (3mm) gap at D for inserting the nose peg (see pattern).

6 Baste the head gusset in place between the head pieces, right sides facing (E – D – E). Stitch, leaving $\frac{1}{8}$in (3mm) holes for the eye pegs (see pattern).

7 Stitch the neck darts on the sides of the head (L – M). Turn the head right side out.

8 Insert the eyes and nose and secure with the washers.

9 Stitch the back arms to the back body (F – G).

10 Stitch the front and back bodies together along the top of the arms (L – F – K). Cut I – H on front and back bodies to form legs.

11 Insert the head into the body cavity, right sides facing, matching points L, C and E. Stitch.

12 Stitch the remainder of the body together leaving an opening on one side for turning.

13 Stitch the darts in the front body piece to shape the arms. Turn the bear right side out.

14 Oversew the heart to the bear's chest.

15 Stuff the head quite firmly. Stuff the body more softly, so that the toy feels 'squashy'. Close the seam with ladder stitches.

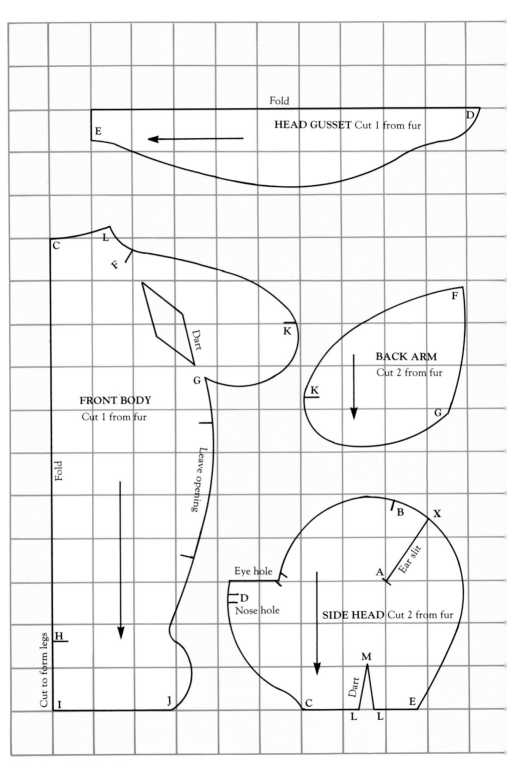

Fold

HEAD GUSSET Cut 1 from fur

E · D

C · L · F

FRONT BODY
Cut 1 from fur

Dart

K

G

Fold

Leave opening

Cut to form legs

H

I · J

F

BACK ARM
Cut 2 from fur

K

G

B · X

A · Ear slit

Eye hole

D
Nose hole

SIDE HEAD Cut 2 from fur

M

Dart

C · L · L · E

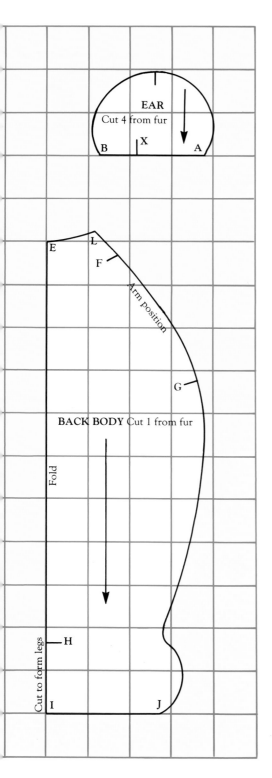

EAR
Cut 4 from fur

B X A

E L
F

Arm position

G

BACK BODY Cut 1 from fur

Fold

Cut to form legs

H

I J

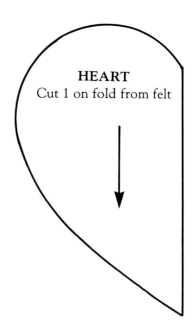

HEART
Cut 1 on fold from felt

Trace this shape on tracing paper.
Cut the heart from folded red felt.

Message bears
The gift of a bear is a perfect way to send your thoughts to someone you love. The message for a Sweetheart bear is simple – just 'I love you' will do. But there are other occasions when a bear can carry a message. 'Thinking of you' might suit a young person about to take important examinations. 'Good luck' suits all kinds of occasions. 'Happy holiday' could be used for any festive occasion.

Children might like to have the bear's name embroidered on the heart – but ask what the name is first – names are very important to children. Or you might use the child's name or initials instead.

A heart shape is an ideal area for working decorative embroidery – such as sprigs of daisy shapes, which would make a very pretty effect.

Tartan twins

Two colourful bears, made from tartan-type fabric, to sit side by side on a shelf or bedside table. Just like a traditional bear, this design has a humped back.

Materials
Squared pattern paper
20in (50cm) of tartan cotton fabric 36in
 (90cm) wide
Pair of eyes for each bear (see note)
Nose for each bear (see note)
Washable polyester toy filling
Ribbon for a bow (optional)

Preparation
1 Draw the graph pattern on squared
graph paper.

2 Put in all words, numerals and marks.
Cut out the pattern pieces.

3 Pin the pattern to the fabric making
sure that matching pieces (head pieces,
arms and legs) have the same area of
pattern on them. Cut out 1 head gusset
on the fold, 4 ear pieces, 2 head pieces,
4 arm pieces, 2 leg pieces on the fold, and
2 body pieces. Reverse pattern pieces as
necessary for right and left sides.

Make sure that pieces have the
same area of pattern on them.

Making the toy

4 Stitch the head pieces together (A – B), leaving a ⅛in (3mm) gap for inserting the nose peg (see pattern).

5 Stitch the ears together in pairs, right sides facing, along the curved edge (D – E). Turn the ears right side out.

6 On the head piece, cut along the line E – D (see pattern). Baste and stitch the ears into these slits.

7 Baste the head gusset in place (B – C – B). Stitch, leaving ⅛in (3mm) gaps in the seams for inserting the eyes (see pattern).

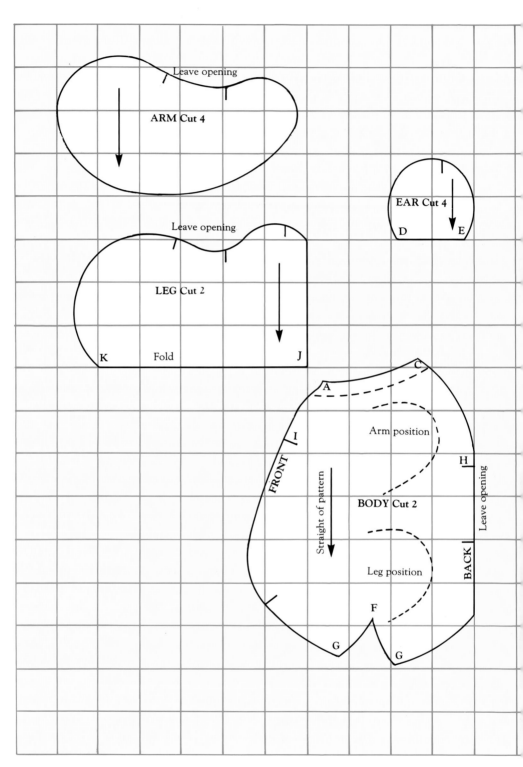

Scale: 1 sq = 1in (2.5cm)

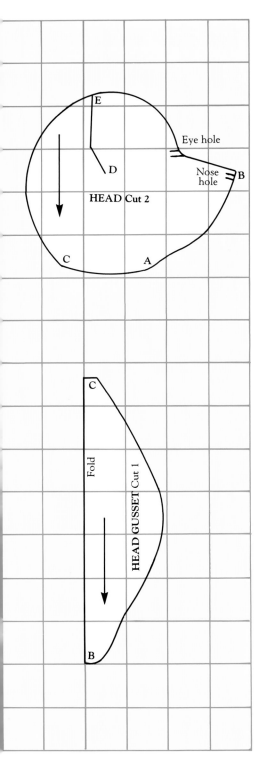

HEAD Cut 2

E

D

Eye hole

Nose hole

B

C A

C

Fold

HEAD GUSSET Cut 1

B

8 Turn the head right side out. Insert the eyes and nose and secure with washers.

9 Stitch the darts F – G on the body pieces. Stitch the body pieces together A – I, C – H.

10 Insert and baste the head into the body cavity, right sides facing, matching A – C – A. Stitch the head to the body.

11 Stitch the body pieces together (H – G – I), leaving an opening in the back for turning. Turn the bear right side out.

12 Arms and legs Stitch arms together in pairs leaving an opening for turning. Turn to the right side.

13 Stitch the legs together (J – K), leaving an opening for turning. Turn right side out.

14 Baste all four limbs to the body (check the pattern for the correct positions). Sew in place using tiny oversewing stitches.

15 Stuff the head, body and limbs very firmly. Close all the seam openings with small ladder stitches.

Note: The look of the bear can be changed by having smaller eyes and nose (see picture).

Baste and oversew the limbs to the body.

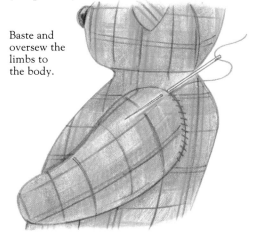

Bedtime bear

A cosy bear-shaped bag that takes a hot water bottle at night, all ready for a cuddle, and doubles as a pyjama or nightie case to lie on the bed during the day.

Materials
Squared pattern paper
2 pieces of rust-coloured felt 36in (90cm) square
18in (45cm) square of orange felt
15in (37.5cm) square of ready-quilted fabric
Small safety nose
Pair of $\frac{3}{8}$in (9mm)-diameter safety eyes
Washable polyester toy filling
Touch-and-hold spots

Preparation
1 Draw the graph pattern on squared pattern paper. Put in all the words, numerals and marks. Cut out the pattern pieces.

2 Pin the pattern to the orange felt and cut out 2 back pieces, 1 front piece on the fold of fabric, 2 foot pads and 2 ear pieces. From rust felt, cut 1 tummy piece on the fold of fabric, 1 muzzle, 2 ear pieces. From quilted fabric cut 1 tummy on the fold of fabric. Transfer the pattern marks to the fabrics.

Making the toy
3 Stitch the rust felt ears to the orange ears along the curved, notched edge (A – B). Turn the ears right side out.

4 Baste the ears in position on the right side of the front piece, making sure that the rust sides face forwards.

5 Stitch the slit in the muzzle leaving a $\frac{1}{8}$in (3mm) hole for the nose peg. Turn the muzzle right side out. Insert the nose and secure with a washer.

6 Sew the muzzle in place with tiny oversewing stitches, leaving a small opening at the base of the muzzle for stuffing. Stuff lightly and close the opening with oversewing.

7 Pierce small holes in the fabric at the eye positions. Insert the eyes and reinforce the fabric round the peg with running stitches. Secure with washers.

8 Trim $\frac{1}{8}$in (3mm) all round from the quilted fabric tummy then baste to the wrong side of the felt tummy shape. Baste to the front of the bear. Oversew in place.

9 Sew the footpads in place with oversewing leaving a small gap for stuffing. Stuff lightly then close the opening with oversewing.

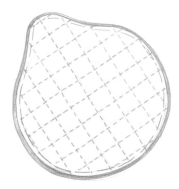

Baste the quilted shape to the wrong side of the felt front body piece.

88

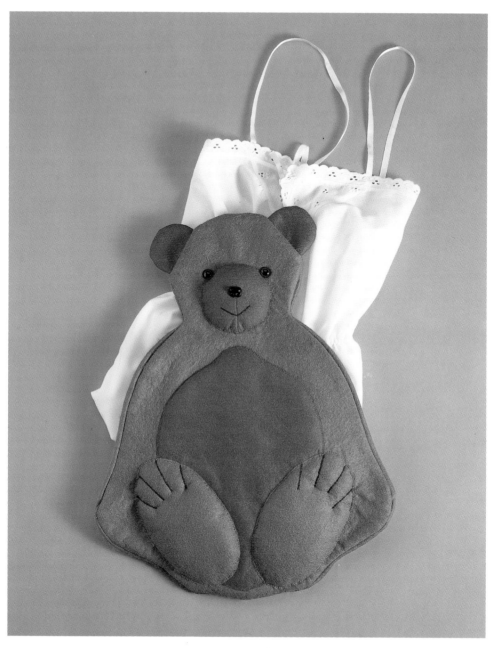

10 Stitch the back pieces together, right sides facing, C – D and E – F. Snip into the seam allowance up to the stitches at D and E.

11 Matching points C and F, stitch front and backs together, right sides facing. Turn right side out.

12 For the back fastenings, sew on touch-and-hold spots.

For a washable bear, trace the pattern onto fabric, work narrow zigzag stitch on the lines. Cut out, baste in place, zigzag stitch the edges.

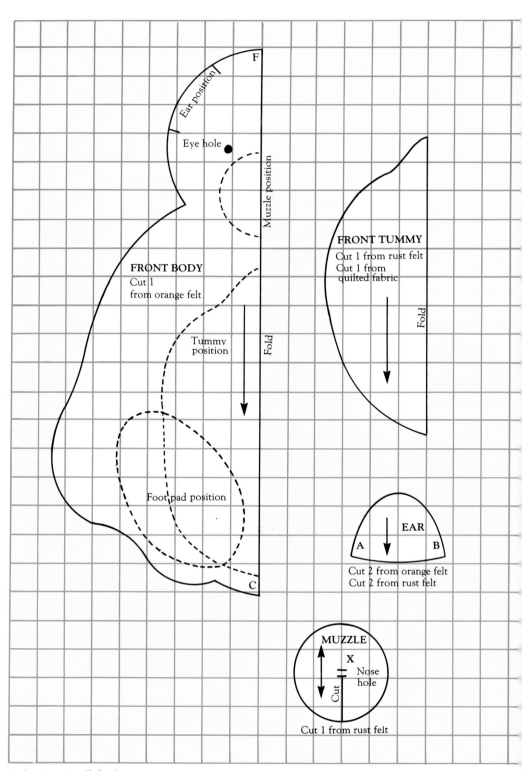

F

Ear position

Eye hole ●

Muzzle position

FRONT BODY
Cut 1
from orange felt

Tummy
position

Fold

Foot pad position

C

FRONT TUMMY
Cut 1 from rust felt
Cut 1 from
  quilted fabric

Fold

EAR

A   B

Cut 2 from orange felt
Cut 2 from rust felt

MUZZLE

X

Nose
hole

Cut

Cut 1 from rust felt

Scale: 1 sq = 1in (2.5cm)

90

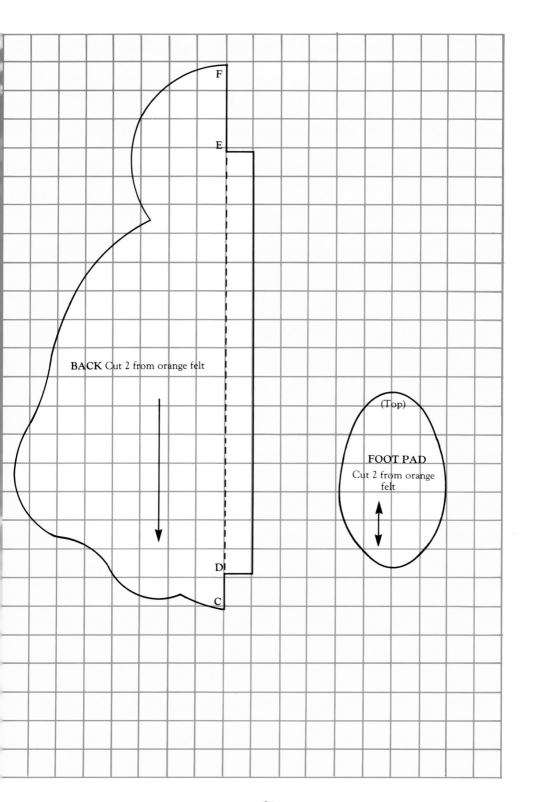

F

E

BACK Cut 2 from orange felt

(Top)

FOOT PAD
Cut 2 from orange
felt

D

C

Get well bear

Here's a sympathetic bear to send to someone who is ill. Tie on a bandage or arm sling, or sew on a felt 'plaster'. Alternatively, tape a written get well message to the bear's front.

Materials
Tracing pattern paper
20in (50cm) of honey-coloured fur fabric 36in (90cm) wide
12in (30cm) square of matching felt
Pair of ¼in (6mm)-diameter amber-coloured safety eyes
Small safety nose
Washable polyester toy filling

Preparation
1 Trace the pattern pieces on pattern paper. Put in all the words, numerals and marks. Cut out the paper pattern pieces.

2 Pin the pattern pieces to the wrong side of the fur fabric, taking note of the directional arrows and reversing pieces for left and right sides.

3 From fur fabric cut out 1 back head and 1 front head on the fold of fabric, 4 ear pieces, 2 back bodies, 1 front body on the fold of fabric. From the felt, cut 1 muzzle on the fold of fabric. Transfer the pattern marks onto the fabrics.

Making the toy
4 Stitch the ears together in pairs, right sides facing, along the curved, notched edge (A – B). Turn the ears right side out.

5 Stitch the darts in the back head piece (H – K). Stitch the darts in the front head pieces (H – K) leaving a ⅛in (3mm) gap where marked for inserting the eyes pegs (see pattern).

6 Baste the ears to the front of the head on the right side in the position marked on the pattern.

7 Stitch the muzzle along L – M, leaving a ⅛in (3mm) hole for inserting the nose peg at M. Turn the muzzle right side out.

8 Insert the nose and secure with a washer. Stitch the front and back heads together, right sides facing (D – K – K – D). Turn right side out.

9 Using tiny oversewing stitches, attach the muzzle to the front of the head in the position indicated leaving a small opening at the base of the muzzle for stuffing. Stuff the muzzle firmly and oversew the opening. Insert the eyes in the head and secure with washers.

10 Stitch up the darts in the front body pieces. Stitch the back body pieces together, right sides facing (C – F) leaving a 3in (7.5cm) opening to turn and stuff.

11 Stitch the front and back body pieces together along the upper arms, right sides facing (D – E).

12 Right sides facing, insert the head in the body cavity and, gathering the stitches slightly, sew the head to the body with back stitches, matching points C, G and D.

13 Stitch the remaining front and back body seams around the limbs and to the base at F.

14 Turn the bear right side out and stuff very firmly. Close the seam with ladder stitches.

15 Dress the bear for presentation as required.

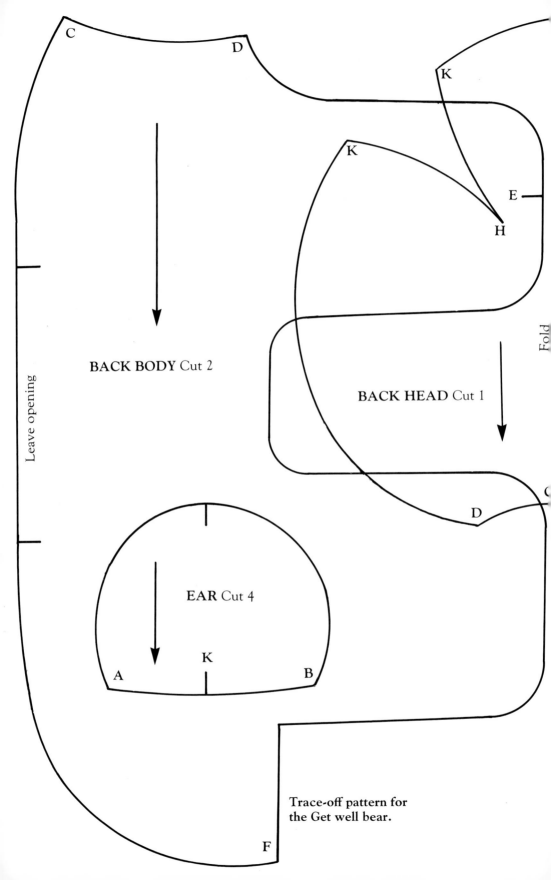

C

D

K

K

E

H

Fold

BACK BODY Cut 2

BACK HEAD Cut 1

Leave opening

D

C

EAR Cut 4

A   K   B

F

Trace-off pattern for
the Get well bear.

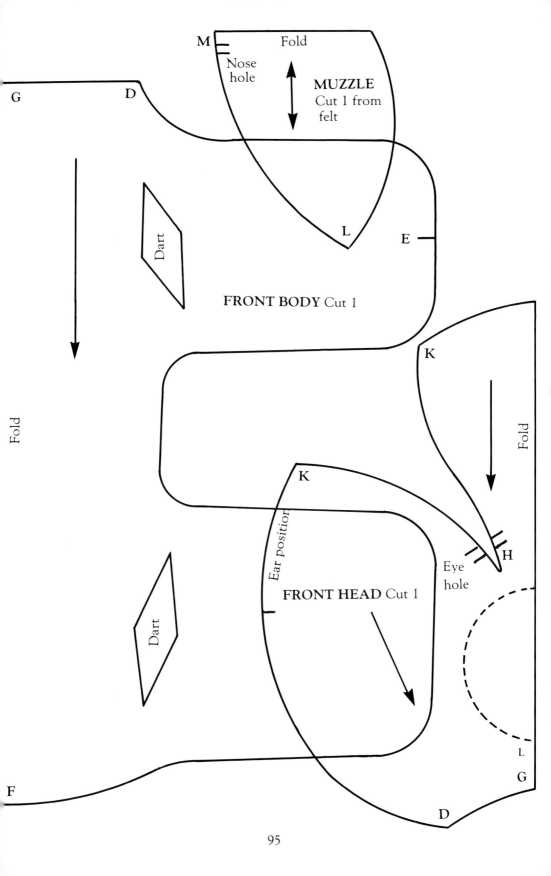

M

Nose hole

Fold

MUZZLE
Cut 1 from felt

G

D

Dart

L

E

FRONT BODY Cut 1

K

Fold

Fold

K

Ear position

H

Eye hole

FRONT HEAD Cut 1

L

G

F

D

Better Techniques

Soft toy-making is just simple sewing and in this chapter you will find all the special techniques you need for making teddy bears – plus some helpful advice on repairing old, worn-out bears.

TOOLS AND EQUIPMENT

If you sew, you will already have most of the basic equipment you need in your work basket. A few special items will help to make the work easier and quicker.

Scissors

A small pair of pointed embroidery scissors is best for cutting fur fabric and felt, and for trimming away pile from muzzles. You will also need a spare pair of scissors to be used only for cutting out paper patterns.

Pins

There are several types available, designed for different uses. For toy-making, use glass or plastic-headed pins with large heads, so that they do not get lost in the fur.

Needles

For hand sewing fur fabrics and felt, use a No. 6 betweens needle. Have several on hand so that a needle can be replaced when it becomes blunt.

If you are machine-stitching, size 14 will suit most fur fabrics, woven fabrics and felt. A larger size will be necessary for thick fur fabrics. If the fur fabric has a knitted back, use a ball-point needle both for hand-sewing and for machine-stitching.

Embroidery needles with a large eye are needed for embroidering noses and mouths. A curved, upholstery needle is useful for sewing hard-to-reach areas.

You may also need an extra long needle for passing threads through toy bodies. A darning needle or bodkin is useful for threading ribbons or elastic through casings.

Sewing machine

A sewing machine is useful for toymaking and a basic model with straight stitch and zigzag stitch facilities is sufficient for your needs. Remember to keep the stitching area clean because fur fabric produces a lot of fluff.

Awl

This is a pointed tool with a handle and is used for making holes in fabric for eyes, noses or for joints. A knitting needle can also be used. Do not use scissors for piercing holes and the tips can cut fabric threads and you may finish up with a hole larger than you need.

Pliers

If you are using joints with split pins, you will need a pair of round-nosed pliers. None of the designs in this book uses joints with split pins but you may meet them when repairing old bears.

Stuffing tools

Stuffing small, narrow areas, such as arms and legs, is a little difficult unless you have a pair of forceps. These can sometimes be found in specialist crafts shops. For other areas, a piece of dowel with the end rounded off with sandpaper, or a chopstick, will suffice.

PATTERN MAKING

Measuring aids

A good tape measure is essential for measuring fabric accurately. Cloth tape measurements can stretch with age so invest in a retractable, plastic-coated measure for accuracy. In this book, measurements are given in both imperial (inches and yards) and in metric (centimetres and metres) and both of these forms are on most tape measures. Choose to work in one of the systems and do not mix them or attempt to convert measurements yourself.

A long ruler and a medium pencil is required for drawing up graph patterns and tracing full-sized patterns.

Squared pattern paper

When patterns are given as graphs, they have to be copied onto squared pattern paper to enlarge them to the correct size. Squared pattern paper is available in different scales. Use the paper that corresponds to the scale quoted on the graph pattern.

Tracing paper

Tracing paper is recommended for tracing same-size patterns but ordinary kitchen greaseproof paper will do just as well.

TRANSFERRING PATTERNS

Patterns are given either as graphs to be enlarged onto squared pattern paper or as direct trace-off patterns. Whichever form the pattern takes, it will have words, numerals and marks on it to guide you in cutting out the fabric and in constructing the toy. All the marks on a pattern should be transferred to the fabric after cutting out. There are different methods of doing this but only three are suitable for fur fabric and felt.

Chalk pencils and coloured pencils

Either of these can be used to draw seam lines, darts, directional arrows, balance marks etc and write words and letters directly onto the wrong side of fur fabric and on felt.

Felt-tipped pens should not be used as the colour may seep through the fabric to the fur side.

Tailor's tacks

Tailor's tacks are the traditional method of transferring pattern marks from pattern to fabric. These are large-looped stitches made at the placement points through both layers of fabric before the pattern is removed.

Use a doubled, contrasting thread and make 3 or 4 large, loose stitches through the paper pattern. Work all the placement points before removing the pattern. Carefully unpin the pattern, gently separate the fabric layers if you are working on doubled fabric, and snip the threads. Thread tufts will be left on both layers of fabric and these are matched before pinning and basting.

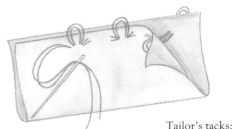

Tailor's tacks:
snip the threads between the layers.

Thread tracing

This is an ideal method when you are working with single layers of fabric. Thread a needle with a contrasting thread. Tie a knot in the end. Work medium-sized running stitches on the stitching line all round the pattern pieces, taking stitches right through the fabric. Outline darts and slit lines, mark eyes and nose placements, balance marks. Tear the pattern away carefully leaving the stitches on the wrong side of the fabric. With pencil, write in all the words and numerals and mark the directional arrows.

The advantage of this method is that you have a line of stitches to help you to machine-stitch straight seams and these can be withdrawn after the work is finished.

Pattern marks

Whether you are drawing up a graph pattern or working from a traced pattern, mark in all the words, numerals and letters on your paper pattern immediately. They are essential to the success of the toy. Then, when the pattern has been pinned to the fabric and cut out, transfer the marks to the fabric.

Names of pieces Each pattern piece has an identifying name (ie front head, back body etc).

Numbers of pieces As well as the name, words and numerals will tell you how many pieces of the pattern to cut out from which fabric and whether one piece should be reversed (ie Front head. Cut 2 from fur fabric, reversing 1).

Directional arrows The paper pattern has directional arrows. When you are pinning the pattern to the wrong side of the fur fabric, make sure the arrows run in the same direction as the pile.

Balance marks In these patterns, balance marks are given as letters.

Dots, spots and lines These generally indicate the positions of eyes and noses.

Fold When this word appears along an edge it indicates that the fabric is to be folded, right sides together and the pattern pinned so that this edge lies along the fold.

Reverse When a pattern specifies two pieces are to be cut to get a left and right hand pieces, cut out one shape then unpin the pattern and flip it over, face down, to get the correct second piece. Be careful that you do not turn it upside down or the fur pile will be lying in the wrong direction.

Seam allowance In this book, seam allowances are included in the patterns and are $\frac{1}{4}$in (6mm) throughout unless otherwise stated.

FURS AND FABRICS

Fur fabrics for toy making are made from man-made fibres, such as nylon, acrylic and modacrylic. Generally they are inexpensive, durable and available in a wide range of textures, piles and colours. Many have a knitted backing so that they are easy to shape when stuffing. Others have a woven backing. Fur fabric for toymaking is usually sold in wide widths so you may only need a short length to make one or two bears. Always check whether the fabric is washable or if it must be drycleaned.

When you are choosing fur fabric, the depth of the pile will be decided by the size of the bear you are making. For instance, a short-pile fur on a big bear will make him seem velvety while a long pile will give the bear a cuddly appearance.

Dressing teddy bears

Some people like to dress their teddy bear and clothes designed for dolls usually suit a bear. However, bears look their best in the minimum of clothes, perhaps just a felt or knitted waistcoat or a pair of knitted dungarees.

Girl bears can be given a skirt or a waistcoat. Small and large bears look cuddly if they have a knitted scarf around the neck.

Big bears can wear neckties or a cravat, or simply a large bow. Smaller bears look better with a bow made of narrow ribbon, or a silky cord. Here is how to make a simple bow tie.

Bow tie

Cut a length of 1in (2.5cm)-wide ribbon, 8in (20cm) long. Join the ends. Cut another small piece of ribbon and sew it around the waist of the bow. Cut a piece of elastic to slip over the bear's head and fit round its neck. Knot the ends and sew the knot behind the ribbon bow.

SEWING STITCHES
Running stitch
A quick and easy stitch, this is used for easing and for gathering. Several stitches can be worked in one go, running the needle in and out of the fabric before pulling the thread through.

Back-stitch
This is a strong stitch that can be used instead of machine-stitching and is often used for seams that are hard to reach with the machine. With right sides of the fabric facing, bring the needle through at A on the the seam line. Take the needle through the fabric about ⅛in (3mm) behind the entry point at B and bring it through to the upper side again about ⅛in (3mm) in front of the entry point at C. Continue, inserting the needle through the left side of the previous stitch and bringing it up a stitch ahead.

Back-stitch.

Gathering
Large, loose running stitches are used to gather up fabrics. Wind the thread ends round vertically-set pins in a figure-of-eight to hold them until the gathering is secured with back-stitches.

Gathering.

Oversewing or overhand stitch
This stitch is used to hold two edges together. Working from right to left, bring the needle through at A and insert the needle from the back of the work at B, bringing it through to the front at C, ready to start the next stitch.

Oversewing.

Slipstitch
This is used to join two folded edges, such as when closing a seam. Working from right to left, bring the needle out through the upper folded edge. Slip the needle through the lower folded edge for about ¼in (6mm). Pull the needle and thread through. Slip the needle through the upper folded edge for about ¼in (6mm). Pull through and continue through the opposite folded edges.

Slipstitch.

Ladder stitch
This is a most important stitch in toy making and is used for closing openings and for attaching ears, limbs etc. It is a simple stitch with the stitches taken first on one side of the opening, then on the other. As you work, turn the seam allowances to the inside with the needle point.

Ladder stitch.

MACHINE STITCHING
Straight stitch is the standard stitch for sewing seams. First, pin and baste the fabric together, right sides facing. Set the machine needle above the seam line and, to begin, work a few stitches backwards and forwards to secure the thread end. Complete the seam in the same way. For fur fabric, you will need a medium stitch length.
Zigzag stitch is often used to neaten seam edges. In toymaking, it is ideal for stitching seams on stretchy jersey fabric.

EMBROIDERY STITCHES

There are literally hundreds of embroidery stitches on record but you will use only a few in toymaking.

Satin stitch

This is often used for working toy eyes and noses. Work stitches evenly and so that they touch. Bring the needle through at A, insert it at B and bring it through again at C.

Satin stitch.

Straight stitch

Straight stitches can also be used for working bear's claws but you will find it most useful for attaching felt eyes. Bring the needle through at A, insert it at B and bring it through again at C.

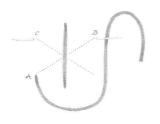

Straight stitch.

Chain stitch

This is a decorative embroidery stitch but in toymaking, it is sometimes used for outlining eyes and noses. As it is a rather bold stitch, chain stitch can be used to work bear's claws.

Chain stitch.

Stem stitch

This stitch is sometimes used for working the line under an embroidered nose and to work the mouth. Bring the needle through at A, the thread below the needle. Insert it at B and bring it through again at C.

Stem stitch.

French knot

In toymaking, French knots are sometimes used to work little eyes on very small bears. You can also use them to highlight felt eyes. Bring the needle through at A, wind the thread round the needle twice and then insert the point at B, close by A. Pull the thread through so that the knot tightens on the fabric surface.

French knot.

Stitch or sew

Toys can be made on a sewing machine or seams can be worked by hand, using back stitch. Instructions will generally say 'stitch' when machine-stitching (or back-stitching) is intended and 'sew' when only hand sewing is required.

MAKING A START
Pattern making
Direct trace-off patterns To use these, you need sheets of tracing paper or kitchen greaseproof paper. Lay the paper over the book page and tape it down at the edges with small pieces of adhesive tape. Trace the image with a sharply-pointed pencil. If you are tracing a multi-pattern, with several pieces overlaid on each other, it may be better to work without taping. Simply trace each individual shape. Put in all the marks, words and numerals as you trace. If there are pieces which require to be reversed for left and right sides (like head sides), it is a good idea to trace both pattern pieces now marking one 'right' and the other 'left'.

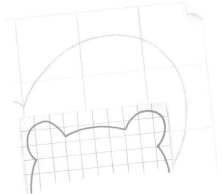

Enlarging a graph pattern.

Half patterns Some patterns are shown as one half only. To make a complete pattern, lay the folded edge of your tracing against the fold line on the master pattern (this will be marked 'place to fold' or 'fold'). Trace the outline, unfold the paper, refold, then trace again.

Lay the folded tracing on the half master pattern, trace and open the tracing for the full pattern.

Direct tracing from the page.

Graph patterns These are given reduced in size on a squared grid. A scale is given and, to produce a full-sized pattern, you need sheets of squared pattern paper.

To reproduce a graph pattern, you copy the lines onto your pattern paper, square for square.

CUTTING OUT
Fur fabric

As fur fabric tends to be thick, it is better to cut pieces from a single layer wherever possible. Before you start, brush your hand along the fur fabric to decide which way the pile is lying and then mark the back of the fabric with a pencilled arrow, the point going along the pile. Your pattern pieces (if you have properly prepared them) will have directional arrows marked also. Arrange the pattern pieces on the wrong side of the fur fabric, matching the arrow directions. You can place pieces quite close together for the patterns in this book as the seam allowance is included. If you are working with patterns where the allowance is to be added, double the allowance and place pieces at least this distance apart.

Pin patterns to fur fabric, making sure that directional arrows follow the pile.

Brush your hand over the fur pile to determine the direction.

Leave the paper pattern pieces in place and do not unpin them completely until you have transferred all the information to the fabric.

Assembling the pieces

Always follow the pattern instructions in the order in which they are given. Pin pieces together first, to make sure that you understand the construction, then baste, before finally machine-stitching (or, if you are working by hand, back-stitching).

Insert pins into the edges of the pattern pieces, lying horizontally to the edges and with the heads just inside the pattern edge. If the fur fabric is too thick to take pins easily without distorting the pattern, use small pieces of sticky tape to hold the pattern down.

Using a small pair of sharply-pointed embroidery scissors, cut out, through the backing only, taking small snips and cutting as little of the pile as possible.

Safety first with pins

When using pins in toymaking, count them as you put them into the pattern or the fabric and make a note. Count them again as you take them out. Always check carefully to ensure that pins are not left hidden in a toy.

SEWING TIPS

Seam allowance In toymaking, almost all the seams are straight seams, where two pieces of fabric are placed together, right sides facing, and are then stitched along the designated seam line, in this book, $\frac{1}{4}$in (6mm) from the fabric edge.

Crossed seam lines When working a seam that is going to be crossed with another line of stitches, stop stitching the width of the seam allowance from the edge. This enables you to make neat corners and seams.

Curved seams After stitching curved seams, clip into the seam allowance to ease the curve so that the seam allowance lies flat.

Clip into curved seams

Layering seams If a crossed seam seems bulky, carefully trim away half of the upper seam allowance but make sure that the seam itself is not weakened.

Trim seam allowance to reduce bulk.

Checking seams In toymaking, it is of utmost importance that the seams are strongly stitched so that stuffing does not seep out. Always check along seams for weak places before stuffing.

Darts Darts are used in toymaking to shape the body or head. To work a dart,

fold the fabric, right sides facing. Baste along the dart line from the widest end to the point. Start stitching at the wide end, using a medium-length stitch. Taper off as you near the pointed end. Fasten off the thread ends securely.

Stitch darts from the wide end.

Fastening thread ends Always make sure that thread ends are securely fastened, whether you are machine stitching or hand sewing. In machine stitching, begin by running the machine backwards and forwards for about $\frac{1}{4}$in (6mm) and then finish in the same way. Alternatively, you can leave long thread ends at the start and finish and tie the threads together tightly. Begin and end hand sewn seams with back-stitches.

Seam finishing Some fabrics tend to fray easily and if you are working with one of these it may be a good idea to oversew the seam edges. Alternatively, a liquid is available from sewing counters that is painted along the cut edges of fabric and virtually prevents fraying from occurring.

Strengthening holes In toymaking, you will often be told to pierce a hole for inserting safety eyes and noses. Always use a sharply pointed tool (such as an awl, or a medium knitting needle). Insert the eye or nose peg, then work small running stitches round the peg to reinforce the fabric.

Trimming pile If the pile of fur fabric is making seams feel thick, trim the pile from the seam allowance after stitching.

Finishing the pile After stitching a seam in fur fabric, work along the seam with a needle point and tease out any strands that have caught in the stitches.

BEARS' FEATURES

Eyes

If you look at old bears, you will see that they have either button eyes or glass eyes on wire stems. You can still buy these types in crafts shops but it is better if you give your bear modern safety eyes made of plastic.

Safety eyes come in different sizes and consist of the eye itself, which is on a peg stem and a washer. The peg is pushed through a hole made in the fabric then the washer is pushed onto the peg to secure the eye. Once secured, eyes cannot be removed or moved so they must be correctly positioned the first time.

Satin-stitched embroidered nose.

Positioning eyes

The most common faults in positioning eyes is setting them too close together or too high and wide apart on the head. The ideal place is about half-way down the head, and not too far apart. The pattern will indicate a dot, spot or lines for the eye positions but it is better to decide the correct place for yourself. To do this, after finishing the head stitching, stuff the head lightly and then cut 2 circles of felt exactly the size of the plastic eyes. Hold the head in your hand and push pins through the felt circles, into the head until you are satisfied that the eyes give the bear exactly the expression you want. Keeping the felt circles pinned, mark the place with a small stitch in coloured thread. Carefully remove the stuffing. Pierce a hole over the marked places and insert the eye pegs. Work tiny running stitches round the peg on the wrong side of the fabric, using a closely matching thread. Remove the contrast marking thread and push the washers onto the pegs.

Plastic safety noses

These come in different shapes and sizes and, like safety eyes, they secured on the inside of the bear with washers.

Embroidered noses

Although plastic noses are easy to apply and are safe to use for children's toys, embroidered noses are always featured on the better quality hand-made bears. The position of the nose will be indicated on the pattern. Cut a nose shape from black felt and try it on the bear to see if the size and position looks right to you. Embroidered noses can be rectangular, square, half-ovals or round-cornered triangles. Pin the felt shape in position.

Once the size and shape of the nose has been decided, shave the pile from the nose area. Using a long needle threaded with wool or embroidery cotton, outline the felt shape with back or stem stitches. Remove the felt and work close, vertical satin stitches to fill the outlined shape. You can work two layers of stitches if you like, to give a well-padded nose.

Fixing the safety eye.

105

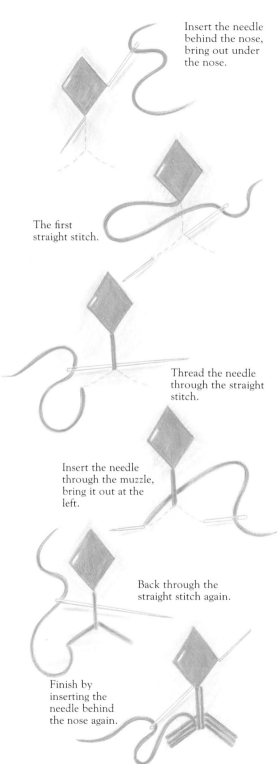

Insert the needle behind the nose, bring out under the nose.

The first straight stitch.

Thread the needle through the straight stitch.

Insert the needle through the muzzle, bring it out at the left.

Back through the straight stitch again.

Finish by inserting the needle behind the nose again.

Mouths

Bear mouths consist of straight stitches, worked in either wool or embroidery cotton, directly under the centre of the nose. The mouth can be worked to be serious or smiling, as you desire, but the basic method of working it is the same.

To decide on the mouth shape, cut some short lengths of wool and pin them under the nose, moving the wool until the look is right. Mark the positions of the wool ends with headed pins. Using a long needle threaded with doubled wool, insert the needle behind the nose and bring it out just under the nose. Insert the needle at the central pin position (remove the pin) and bring it out at the left-hand pin position (remove the pin). Take the needle back under the straight, vertical stitch just made and then into the right-hand pin position (remove the final pin). Bring the needle out at the left-hand pin position again, passing the needle through the muzzle. Take the needle under the straight stitch again and back into the right-hand pin position, up behind the straight stitch again and pass the needle behind the nose one or twice to secure the wool end.

Muzzle If you like the effect, you can trim the fur pile from the bear's muzzle. This if particularly necessary when the fur has a long pile. Brush the pile with your fingers or with a comb so that it stands up and then snip the pile with small scissors, very carefully, so that it is evenly short over the muzzle area.

Stuffing

Washable, polyester toy filling is the best for new toys. It can be packed in for a firm body or loosely for a squashy feel. Sawdust is sometimes used by traditionalists who want to reproduce the old, traditional bears. If you are one of these, use only clean, dry sawdust without splinters in it.

JOINTED BEARS
Plastic joints are mostly used in toys intended to be washable. Joints consist of two plastic discs, one of which has a stem or peg and the other has a hole to fit the stem. The two discs are secured with a washer.

Fitting a joint
The position of a joint will be marked on the pattern pieces for the limb and the body. To mark this on the unstuffed toy, push the hole disc inside the limb and check the position, marking it with pencil or a small stitch. Remove the disc. Pierce a hole on the mark. Now put the disc with the peg inside the limb and push the peg through the hole.

Push the holed disc into the toy body and check the position. Mark the place and pierce a hole.

To ensure that the joints fit well and do not hang loosely, it is a good idea to trim the fur pile from the surfaces where the limbs touch the body. Trim away the fur. Push the disc peg through the hole in the body and push the hole disc onto it. Slip the washer onto the stem or peg and press the joint together very firmly with your fingers.

STUFFING TOYS
Stuffing soft toys is an art and care should be taken at this most important stage. Always use a good quality, washable polyester toy filling. Follow the pattern instructions for the correct order in which to stuff the toy. The secret is to tease out the filling and insert only small pieces at a time.

The pattern instructions will tell you whether the toy is to be stuffed firmly or whether the finished toy is to feel 'squashy' and cuddly. Whatever the density of the filling, it should be even and without lumpy places. You may need a pair of forceps to push stuffing into small areas (specialist crafts shops should be able to supply these). Otherwise, use a chopstick or a blunt pencil to push the stuffing into place.

If the stuffing needs to be rearranged, a

Sewing with felt
When cutting felt to shape, cut it out in the same way as when working with fabric, by pinning the paper pattern to it. Marking on felt is best done with tailor's tacks. When you are cutting out small shapes, such as bear's paw pads, either iron the felt onto bonding interfacing or press the felt onto a small, self-adhesive label. This helps you to cut out with a firm edge. Remove the paper label afterwards. Felt can be machine-stitched or hand-sewn with running stitches or back-stitches.

long, thin upholstery needle with double-pointed ends is inserted into the fabric and the tip moved around until the stuffing is redistributed to your liking.

After stuffing, close open seams with ladder stitches.

Toymaker's tip To ensure that the joint is firmly fitted together, slip an empty cotton thread spool onto the protruding peg (it should not fit tightly). Lay the joint on a flat surface and give the thread spool two or three taps with a hammer. Lift off the spool.

Eye ideas for toys

1. Eye embroidered in satin stitch

2. Straight stitches over a felt circle

3. Felt circle with a chain stitch outline

4. Pie slice eye in felt

5. Felt circle with straight stitch eyelashes

6. Button eye and stem stitch eyelashes

7. Straight stitch cross eye

Making a stuffing tool

If you are making a number of stuffed toys, a proper stuffing tool is an advantage. Cut a piece of ½in (1cm)-diameter dowelling about 12in (30cm) long. Shape one end to a rough point with a crafts knife. Smooth the point with sandpaper.

Eye effects

You may like to try the effect of darkening the fur round your bear's eyes. This can give the effect of soft modelling. Use brown or grey fabric paint and mix it, fairly dry, according to the manufacturer's instructions. With soft, light brush strokes, brush colour onto the fur strands around the eyes. Work slowly and take care not to apply too much colour. The aim should be to darken the fur around the eyes and thus make them stand out.

Check list

Tracing paper
Squared pattern paper
Pencils
Measuring tape
Ruler
Fur fabrics
Felt
Cutting out scissors
Paper scissors
Crafts knife
Dressmakers carbon paper
Dressmakers chalk pencil
All-purpose adhesives
Glass or plastic-headed pins
Sewing needles
Sewing thread
Embroidery needles
Embroidery wool
Stranded embroidery cotton
Washable polyester toy filling
Stuffing tool
Plastic safety eyes
Plastic safety nose

OTHER SOFT TOYS
Faces and features
In soft toy making, the features are probably the most important stage because clumsy work can spoil the toy's appearance. A child can become completely averse to a toy whose face he thinks is unattractive or menacing. If eyes, for instance, are set too close together, or too high on the head, the toy can look bad tempered. Big, black eyes, without highlight or other decoration, sometimes look staring and hypnotic.

Always plan the positions of eyes, noses and mouths before starting embroidery or sticking on pieces of felt. Mark the desired positions with chalk pencil – the marks will brush away afterwards – or with tiny stitches in contrasting thread, which can be unpicked.

For most soft toys, especially dolls, embroidered features are best because they last and cannot be accidentally pulled off during play.

Eyes
If eyes are being embroidered directly onto a toy's face it is often easier to do this before stuffing the head, when you can still get your hand inside. However, work after stuffing, if you find this suits you better. There are various ways of working eyes, depending on the character of the toy and the expression you want to achieve.

Embroidered eyes
Work the entire eye in satin stitch, using 2 strands of stranded embroidery cotton in the needle. Work the eyeball in white or cream, the iris in blue or brown, and the pupil in black. Make sure that the stitches are even and touching, so that a smooth surface is achieved. A highlight can be added to the pupil with a white French knot. If you like, work straight stitch eyelashes radiating from the upper eyelid afterwards.

Felt eyes
Felt is the most popular material for eyes and all kinds of expressions can be achieved quite easily. For a basic eye, cut a circle of white felt (use a coin for a template), then another of darker coloured felt, but a little smaller. Glue the dark circle to the light, then, when it is dry, hem all round the edges to secure the dark circle in position. Sew the assembled eye to the toy's face.

The darker circle can be placed to the left or to the right of the white circle to give the effect of the toy looking sideways. Always make sure that both eyes are looking in exactly the same direction when you sew them on.

Pie-slice eyes
These look effective and are very easy to make. Cut 2 white circles and 2 black, of the same size. Cut a slice from the black circles. Glue, then stitch the black circles on the white, making sure that the slice is at the same angle on both eyes. Sew the eyes to the toy's face.

Noses
Soft, animal toys will usually have animal noses, cut from felt or embroidered on the face. On soft dolls, the nose is just a few stitches in stem stitch. If a more pronounced nose is required, cut a circle of the face fabric, gather up the edges and stuff with a little toy filling. Sew to the doll's face with ladder stitches.

Mouths
If these are to be embroidered, work them in stem stitch, straight stitch or chain stitch, using 2 strands of embroidery cotton. Use a suitable colour for the toy being made. Black or brown is usually best for animals, red for dolls.

Remember that a curved line will always give a toy a happier expression.

> ### Pretty eyes
> When embroidering eyes on a doll, work on the stuffed face and position the eyes a little higher than half-way down the face and widely spaced.

BEAR CARE

Inevitably, a teddy bear is going to get grubby, especially if he has a young owner and is played with a great deal. If the fur and stuffing is washable, and the eyes are plastic safety eyes, the bear can probably be put into a washing machine at a low-medium temperature. It is best to put the toy into a pillow case first and tie the top. Afterwards, the bear will usually be alright in a tumble dryer but take the precaution of again tying it into a pillow case and set the machine for fine fabrics.

It is inadvisable to wash bears with growler mechanisms inside or old bears, which may have wood chip or straw filling, or cardboard joints. The safest way to handle old bears is to wash the fur, by hand, with mild soap suds and a sponge or soft brush. Lay the bear on a large towel, dip the sponge in the suds and then work in a circular motion, without getting the bear really wet. Wipe the suds away with a damp cloth and dry the bear with a hair-dryer. Comb the fur while you are drying with a dog comb – but always work very gently or you may damage the pile of the toy.

First aid for bears

Eyes The most common repair a toy bear requires is a missing eye. Modern bears, with plastic safety eyes, rarely lose an eye. Older bears may have wire-mounted eyes and, with wear, these can drop out.

It will be almost impossible to match the remaining eye, unless you are lucky enough to discover one in a collector's shop. It is better to look for a pair of eyes, that are more or less the right size, and that have a ring on the back. First, remove the remaining eye.

You will need a long, toymaker's needle (or an upholstery needle) and strong button thread. Slip the thread through the eye ring. Bring the ends level and thread the ends through the needle eye. Push the needle into the eye placement, right through the head and out again behind the nearest ear, towards the middle of the top of the head. Take one of the threads back through the head and out at the other eye placement. Thread on the eye and take the needle back through the head and out behind the nearest ear. Pull the threads tightly to settle the eyes, then tie the threads ends in a double knot, very tightly. Trim the ends and the knot should be hidden in the fur.

Apply suds with a sponge or soft brush, working in a circular motion.

Bring the needle out behind the ear, on the head.

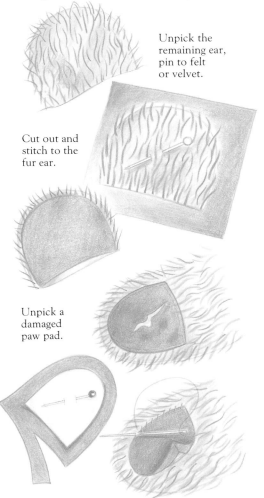

Unpick the remaining ear, pin to felt or velvet.

Cut out and stitch to the fur ear.

Unpick a damaged paw pad.

Tuck the edges of the felt under the fur edges and sew in place.

Split seams First, push the stuffing back into the hole, using a blunt, thick knitting needle. Using a sewing thread that closely matches the fur colour, close the seam with slipstitches, working close to the seam edges. Make sure you begin and end with 2 or 3 back-stitches.

If the damage is a hole rather than a broken seam, the fur fabric may be worn on the edges. Turn the hole edges under and pull them together with ladder stitches.

Ears If the ear is just hanging off, it is a simple matter to pin the ear back in place then sew it in place with tiny, oversewing stitches. A missing ear presents a bigger problem. Remove the remaining ear and turn it inside out. Carefully unpick the stitches holding front and back together. Use one piece as a pattern and cut the shape from felt or velvet. Re-make the ears, so that they each have a felt or velvet front and a fur back. Turn the ears right side out and turn in the raw edges. Oversew, then sew the new ears to the bear's head.

Paw pads This is a tricky repair job and, if possible, it is better to mend holes and slits in pads before they get too large. Cut a piece of light-weight felt, similar in colour to the original pad. With small, sharply-pointed scissors, carefully cut away the old pad. Use this as a pattern to cut the new pad from felt, cutting it about ⅜in (9mm) larger all round. Position the felt pad over the hole. Using a thin knitting needle, push the edges of the felt under the fur edges. Sew in place with tiny oversewing stitches. Comb the fur back over the seam.

Fabrics for bear making
Upholstery plush is a good fabric for most bears. Mohair-type fabrics are suitable and upholstery velvet can also be used. Dressmaking fabrics (brushed cotton, polyester cotton in patterns and plains, velveteens, needlecord, towelling and cotton velour) can all be used for some types of bears.

Useful addresses

Fur fabrics and joints, eyes, noses, etc
from branches of John Lewis Partnership.

Fur fabrics and toy-making accessories
from Fred Aldous Ltd, Manchester.

Fabrics from Oakley Fabrics Ltd, 8 May
Street, Luton, Beds, LU1 3QY.
Tel: 0582 34733.